CALLWEY

IGOR JOSIFOVIC
JUDITH DE GRAAFF

URBAN JUNGLE

LIVING
AND STYLING
WITH PLANTS

WITH PHOTOGRAPHS BY LINA SKUKAUSKÈ
AND ILLUSTRATIONS BY SAAR MANCHE

CALLWEY

EDITORIAL 7

AT HOME WITH

MARIJ & EVERT 8

DIY
DIY Hanging planter
22

PLANT PORTRAITS

Cactus plants 24
Succulents 28
Aloe Vera 34

DIY
Growing succulents
32

STYLING TIPS 36

AT HOME WITH

JESKA & DEAN 46

PLANT PORTRAITS

Monstera Deliciosa 60
Oxalis triangularis 64

DIY
Terrarium
57

STYLING TIPS 68

AT HOME WITH

DIY
Plant stand
86

PEPPER, MICHAEL & NAHELE 72

PLANT PORTRAITS

Ficus elastica 88
Calathea 92

STYLING TIPS 96

AT HOME WITH

MORGANE & ARMAND 102

DIY
Botanical frame
118

PLANT PORTRAITS

Tradescantia 120
Pilea peperomioides 124

STYLING TIPS 128

AT HOME WITH

FEM, SAN & SEZER 134

DIY
Kokedama
150

PLANT PORTRAITS

Palms 152
Sansevieria 156

STYLING TIPS 160

PLANTS AT HOME
YOUR OWN URBAN JUNGLE 166

URBAN JUNGLE BLOGGERS IN THE BOOK 170

OUR FAVOURITE SHOPS FOR
PLANT LOVERS 172

ACKNOWLEDGMENTS 174
COLOPHON 176

GET INSPIRED, GET INFORMED AND GET GOING – "URBAN JUNGLE"
IS MORE THAN A COFFEE-TABLE BOOK. IT IS THE BEST
AND MOST WONDERFUL WAY OF LIVING AND DWELLING.
HERE'S TO PLANTS!

EDITORIAL

URBAN JUNGLE – LIVING AND STYLING WITH PLANTS

Everything started back in 2013 with a chat between two friends in a Parisian café. Over coffee, we talked about interior styling, our love for redecorating and about plants. It was right there and then that we discovered our common passion: our love for plants.

We quickly came up with the idea of choosing a green topic each month and interpreting it through plant styling on our blogs. After the first month we had other bloggers asking to join us. Over the following months even more plant enthusiasts joined, and today, three years later to be precise, the Urban Jungle Bloggers community unites more than 1,200 plant enthusiasts and bloggers around the globe, from all over Europe, the United States, Brazil and even New Zealand.

The book "Urban Jungle" is like a long-awaited cactus flower. For three years we have been creating green living ideas with our community. We have peeked into hundreds of urban jungles all around the world, we have appraised unusual plant styling ideas and we have exchanged plant care tips. The moment has finally come to pack all of this green creativity into one book. The result is in your hands right now.

In "Urban Jungle" we will take you on an inspiring voyage across Europe to five green homes, taking a closer look at these creative people's houseplants and chatting with them about plants, plant care and green styling ideas. Count on us: we will uncover their secrets

and tips for you! Moreover, we have invited a group of amazing members of our Urban Jungle Bloggers community to showcase their plant styling ideas, DIY projects and green vignettes. But this publication is way more than just an inspiring coffee-table book to flip through: it also includes ten plant portraits and simple plant-care tips. It is no botanical encyclopedia – it is a book for everyone who wants to bring more green into their home, no matter whether they are a beginner or an expert. We do not believe in the concept of the so-called "green thumb". We prefer to believe that anyone can live with and care for plants. All you need is the right information – and this book is a first step in the right direction.

On this note: get inspired, get informed and get green with your own plant styling at home. "Urban Jungle" is more than just a book – it is a one-way ticket to your own lush, dreamy urban jungle. Here's to plants!

IGOR & JUDITH
urbanjunglebloggers.com

MARIJ & EVERT

Alphen aan den Rijn / The Netherlands

FRESHNESS NEAR AMSTERDAM

In the middle of the "Green Heart" of the Netherlands, close to tulip fields, greenhouses
and windmills, Marij and Evert live with their two cats and 50 plants. While the surroundings of
Alphen aan den Rijn may be as ordinarily Dutch as can be, this creative couple's home
is atypical and contemporary.

⌄ *Together with their two cats, Def and Mos (not pictured), Marij and Evert live in a cosy and colourful home in the green heart of Holland.*

Marij runs her own online shop for vintage and upcycled furniture and ceramics, and also works as a fashion stylist, photographer and blogger, while Evert works as a visual merchandiser for a fashion brand. The couple's sense of style can be felt in every room: there's not a single corner that looks dull or messy. And any time Marij thinks a room needs a bit of pep, she reaches for paint and brush and isn't afraid to add a graphic shape to the wall – in mint or palm green for example. Her latest splash is the dusty pink wall in the dressing room, which complements the camel-coloured accessories and the deep green of the Alocasia and Euphorbia triangularis so well.

I FIND A LOT OF NICE PLANT POTS AT THRIFT SHOPS. I COMBINE THEM WITH NEW MODERN POTS FROM THE GARDEN CENTRE.

SEE PAGE 92

< Marij painted the vintage chest in a pale pink for some #plantsonpink perfection.

∧ The linear details of the artwork are reflected by the pink line pattern on the leaves of the Maranta leuconeura erythroneura.

ⱽ *A hanging Rhipsalis, a fern, succulents and a cactus are joined by some vintage friends from the African jungle.*

IT'S NOT THE END OF
THE WORLD IF YOU
KILL A PLANT. IT'S AN
EXCUSE TO CHOOSE A
NEW ONE!

< *The bathroom has been turned into a lush spa retreat with ferns and two aloe vera plants.*
∟ *In the attic of the house, Marij collects vintage furniture, ceramics and dinnerware that she sells online in her shop My Attic and at markets and festivals.*
∨ *Contemporary ceramics stand side by side with vintage plant pots.*

Under the roof, on the second floor, Marij has created a treasure trove: her attic. With a passion for vintage designs and an eye for style, she sources the best vintage ceramics and furniture at flea markets and thrift stores in Holland, Germany, Belgium and France. She then upholsters the pieces of furniture with contemporary fabrics (from Febrik) and paints them in pale pink, ochre or mint. To show her clients and blog readers that vintage designs can add some serious style to a contemporary home, she combines her finds with modern objects from design shops and independent designers.

Marij cannot visit a nursery or garden centre without taking home a new green friend. And even though their home has nearly 50 plants, it does not look like an out-of-control jungle. She dispatches the plants to every room of the home, including the bathroom. The Bird's nest fern (Asplenium nidus) in there thrives with the humid air and limited amounts of sunlight. To prevent the home from looking too full-on "planty", Marij likes to add

DID YOU KNOW

that most Rhipsalis cacti droop, but some are upright or sprawling? They add a different texture to your cactus mix.

⌐ *This Phlebodium pseudoaureum, also known as Blue Star Fern, is an easy houseplant. He thrives in indirect light with good drainage, and he also likes to be misted, especially when humidity is low.*

∧ *Vintage furniture mixed with a big contemporary hanging lamp, modern cups and a thrifted cactus mug.*

COOL IDEA

Creating your own plant hanger is very easy. Use some beautiful strings, ribbons or rope made of fabric or natural fibres to knot your hanger (see instructions on page 22). To make a plant hanger more personal, you can embellish it with shells that you've collected during a holiday. Before knotting the strings together, thread the shells onto them and then glue larger shells onto the knots.

smaller botanical details to the walls and shelves, like a vintage cactus photo, terrarium illustrations or artificial gold cacti. There's botanical inspiration everywhere.

One of Marij's tips is to suspend plants from the ceiling in easy-to-make plant hangers: this creates a nice dynamic in the room without taking up precious floor space. With some rope and shells or beads, you can knot your own plant hanger (DIY tutorial on page 22). For the hallway she used rope and paint to create a hanging hexagonal wooden shelf which welcomes guests with a hanging ivy. And as a bonus for cat owners, this keeps the plant out of reach of plant-destroying furry friends. Def and Mos could not care less about the plants, though – they much prefer cuddles and sunbathing.

> The home office is also decorated with plants, both real and in glossy white ceramics. Vintage coffee cups are nice vessels for small cacti and succulents.

GREEN HAS ALWAYS BEEN MY
FAVOURITE COLOUR. FROM PALE
MINTY GREEN TO FRESH GRASS
GREEN AND DEEP DARK
FOREST GREEN

< Minimal effort, maximum style: create your own plant shelf with a plank, two leather belts and some jam jars.

∨ The wall of the dressing room was painted in a peachy pink, which makes the deep green of the Alocasia amazonica plants pop. Illustrated terrariums by Inge from Teken-ing add a soft botanical touch to this corner.

∨ It looks like cactus, but it's a succulent. This Euphorbia trigona is also known as African Milk tree because of the milky white sap that streams from the plant when cut. The latex from the plant is poisonous and can cause skin irritations.

SEE PAGE 28

COOL IDEA

Cups, mugs and small vases can be turned into plant pots. Because you don't want to destroy your ceramics by drilling drainage holes in the bottom, be sure to fill the bottom layer with clay drainage balls, little pebbles or some terracotta shards that will create space for excess water. Small cacti or succulents are particularly suited for this kind of container, as they like their soil to be dry in between waterings.

When shopping for new plants, Marij looks for unexpected shapes and colours, as well as graphic details and patterns that match their interior. The two big Calathea plants in the living room create a striking contrast with the pink chest. Marij also fell in love with the pink details of the Herringbone plant (Maranta tricolour), for which she painted an Ikea Ingefära plant pot. Decorated plant pots are a staple in Marij and Evert's home: as with their interior design, they create a mix of vintage, painted and DIY pots. After leaving Marij and Evert's beautiful home, you can be sure of one thing: Netherland's "Green Heart" is truly beating strong in Alphen aan den Rijn.

→ *Find out more about Marij at entermyattic.com*

PLANTS ADD A FRESH TOUCH TO YOUR INTERIOR. IT'S SO NICE TO BRING NATURE INSIDE, AND I LOVE USING PLANTS IN STYLING PROJECTS FOR MY BLOG. IT ADDS THAT LITTLE EXTRA TO A PHOTO.

↗ *Cacti in vintage hat plant pot and in a specked teacup and saucer.*
> *A vintage typewriter and secretary dress up the corner next to the daybed where Def loves to sleep (he shares with guests).*

⌄ With plants on different floors of the house, Marij has several watering cans at hand to make plant watering an easy chore.

5 QUESTIONS
FOR MARIJ

1 **Living with plants – is this a lifestyle choice or the natural way of life in your home?**

For me it's not a conscious choice. This way of life grew over the years, and I started enjoying having plants at home more and more. I cannot imagine our home without them anymore. I like to place a group of plants in every room, and we actually do have some green in every room.

2 **How would you describe the style of your home?**

I would describe my interior as a mix of eclectic, Scandinavian design, vintage, graphic elements and prints, fresh pastels and a hint of boho. I don't know if you could put a label on my style – I follow my gut feeling and when I like something, I combine it with the things I already have. This creates an exciting mix, I think. I also love colour. At the moment my favourites are ochre yellow, minty green and pale pink, combined with lots of white. My vintage finds really pop against this colour palette. And of course, there's always a huge amount of green!

3 **You have a beautiful collection of plants at home. How did it grow over time?**

When I'm looking for new plants, I mainly look at shapes and structures. Every time I am surprised by what nature has designed. The leaves of some plants have beautiful lines that look just like prints. I regularly discover new kinds of plants that I have never seen before – there's a lot of innovation in the plants on offer at shops. My plant collection has grown over the years. I started with a cactus, because they are so easy to care for and because they were so trendy. Fortunately, this green trend is here to stay and I don't think it will disappear anytime soon.

4 **Do you have a favourite plant at home? If so, why?**

I have one fairly big Euphorbia which was one of my first plants, so he's been with us for quite a while. This makes him extra special. Unfortunately, he doesn't really grow. I wouldn't mind if he became big and tall.

5 **How do you care for your plants?**

Quite naturally, I try to water my plants regularly. To make watering all our plants more easy and efficient, I have a watering can at hand on both floors. I've learned that every plant needs a different kind of care, and I usually just touch the soil to find out if it needs water. Also, I regularly remove old leaves, because they deplete the plant's energy.

STYLING TIP

Combine plants with different shapes, sizes and structures: this intensifies the effect. A beautiful mix of different kinds of plant pots, like vintage, retro and more contemporary ones, also works really well. If you use one colour palette for all your planters, it creates a sense of unity.

HANGING PLANTERS

Even if you don't have any space left on your shelves or the windowsill, there's always room for a hanging plant. You can hang it from the ceiling, a wall or a window or doorknob that isn't used on a daily basis.

∧ *Regular plant pots, like terracotta pots, work very well for macramé hangers. But salad bowls that are round on the bottom also look good.*

DO IT YOURSELF

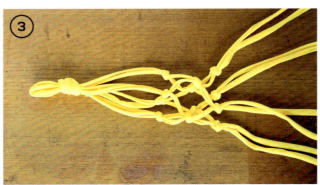

(1) *Start with four 3-metre lengths of fabric yarn. Fold them in the middle and tie them all together in one knot, keeping a little loop. You should now have eight strings to work with. For the next step, it helps if you attach the loop to a nail in the wall or to a doorknob.*

(2) *Divide the strings in four groups of two. Tie a simple knot in each pair at 40 cm below the main loop knot. You will have four knots that line up horizontally. Make sure each knot is tight.*

(3) *Take one string from two adjacent knotted pairs, and tie them together in a knot about 8–10 cm below the previous knot. Repeat this until all of the bundles are tied together. This creates a zig-zag pattern among the strings.*

(4) *Tie all eight lengths together with a small tie cut from the same fabric yarn, or make one large final knot with all the strings. Pull each string individually to ensure that the knot is as tight as possible. Use scissors to trim the strings to your desired length. You can add beads or ribbons for added style and texture.*

For this tutorial we used an old cotton T-shirt to create fabric yarn. One T-shirt is enough for one plant hanger. Lay your T-shirt flat on a table and cut off the sleeves with a pair of scissors. Then start at the bottom and cut all around the T-shirt in a spiral, with a width of 15–20 mm. Continue until you reach the sleeves. You now have one very, very long thread. You will see that the fabric curls up nicely when you gently pull it.

CACTUS PLANTS

Together with succulents, cactus plants seem to be everywhere: in that hip boutique around the corner, on the table in your favourite café, on the windowsill at your friend's. Or maybe you even have some cacti yourself. Of course there's a reason why cactus plants enjoy such popularity: they are easy to care for (not maintenance-free, though!) and come in all kinds of colours and shapes: hairy, columnar, with "bunny ears" or cushiony.

< *Cactus plants look great in photos – and next to vintage cameras too!*

> *For a cactus setting with a retro vibe, without being full-on 1970s, look for vintage ceramics with sleek contemporary shapes.*

Don't be fooled into thinking that a cactus is a cactus just because it has spines. There are many species of succulents with spines that aren't in the Cactaceae family, such as some Euphorbias and Agaves. Also, some cacti – like most Lophophoras, for example – don't have spines at all. All cacti are succulents, but not all succulents are cacti.

What defines true cacti are areoles. Areoles are what spines, glochids (barbed spines), branches and flowers sprout from, and all cacti have them, while succulents other than cacti do not. Areoles are not hard to find: they usually look like small, fluffy, cotton-like bumps on the body of the cactus.

Many people envision cactus plants growing in Sahara Desert sands with practically no water, but that's a misconception.

CACTI ARE REAL EYE-CATCHERS IN SMALL GROUPS OR COMBINED WITH OTHER HOUSE PLANTS AS A PLANTGANG.

Their reputation for getting by without water comes from their ability to survive in dry areas where little water is available or where water is delivered infrequently. In reality, water is essential for all cacti to live! The key to healthy, thriving cacti isn't in avoiding watering, but in being sure not to overwater your plants.

There are actually two kinds of cacti. Desert cacti are the ones that come to mind when you hear the word "cactus". These cacti hail from the arid regions of the Americas and their surrounding islands. However, there are also jungle cacti, which grow in tropical rain forests and other environments that you would expect to be completely unsuitable for a cactus plant. Jungle cacti originate from the tropical jungles in Central and South America and mostly grow in trees or on rocks. The most common jungle cacti are the Christmas cactus and the Rhipsalis.

OUCH, THOSE SPINES HURT!

In the wild, cactus spines act as a defence mechanism against herbivores, and they also help prevent water loss by reducing air flow close to the cactus. In our homes, the spines are sometimes a bit tricky. A tip for repotting your cactus plants without needing to use tweezers afterwards: wrap your cactus in a few glossy magazine pages. Then carefully move the cactus from the old pot to the new one. Be especially careful when manipulating a cactus with glochids, those tiny hairy spines: they are irritating and barely visible to the eye, which means they are difficult to remove. If necessary, you can use duct tape to remove glochids from your skin.

Despite their prickly features, cacti are great houseplants for everyone from beginners to advanced gardeners. Very few other plants need such little attention and care while bringing unlimited sculptural style to any room in your home. Cacti are true eye-catchers, in both small groups and larger plantgangs.

∨ *The difference between cacti and succulents: the areoles, small, fluffy, cotton-like bumps on the body of a cactus.*
> *Cacti require only small amounts of water, so you can keep them in tea or coffee cups without drainage holes (use clay drainage balls on the bottom).*

DID YOU KNOW

that while cactus plants do add lots of happiness and beauty to a home, they don't have air-cleaning properties? Nevertheless, they are perfect green roommates!

CARE TIPS:

Location: Place cacti close to the window; they need a maximum amount of sunlight.

Temperature: Anything goes, as long as they are protected from frost.

Watering: During the growth period (spring to autumn), water cacti abundantly, until water runs out of the pot. Don't leave water standing in the pot or saucer, and wait until the soil is completely dry before watering again. Cacti can (and will) start to rot when you overwater.

April - October: For a cactus plant in a pot with a diameter of <5 cm, water every 3 to 8 days, depending on temperature and sun exposure. For pots with a diameter of >30 cm, water every 10 to 20 days.

November - March: Water less than in summer. For a cactus plant in a pot with a diameter of <5 cm, give a small cup of water every 1 to 2 weeks, depending on temperature. For pots with a diameter of >30 cm, give a litre of water every 2 to 4 weeks.

Most cacti don't need fertilizer. During the growth period, however, you can add liquid fertilizer every two to four weeks when watering.

SUCCULENTS

Succulents really need no introduction: they are among the most popular
and easy plants out there. They do come in many different varieties, from graphic-looking
Echeverias, with their large rosettes of thick leaves, to tall cactus-like species.

S ucculents are plants that store water in their leaves and stems so that they can tolerate dry conditions. Most of them have thick leaves and stems that act as water storage tanks, but many succulents can also reduce water loss through transpiration due to their waxy leaves or thin layer of hair.

Echeverias are hard to resist when shopping. Not only do they come in all different kinds of colours, but they are very decorative (which is especially appealing if you are shooting tabletop pictures for Instagram, *wink wink*) and very affordable, too. The plants usually look really nice when we purchase them, but watch out – they often change their shape and colour in the following weeks and months.

⌐ *Small decorated cups and vases are perfect for Echeveria succulents and a mini cactus.*

> *Go wild! Here, plant pots and a glass dome are mixed and matched, and a String of Pearls plant grows from a drawer.*

< Some succulents, like certain kinds of Sedum, turn red to protect themselves from the cold or too much sun. A natural sunscreen!

V This Senecio rowleyanus grows in a glass plant hanger with a leather strap.

> If you are lucky, your succulent will bloom. Create optimum conditions by letting your plant hibernate at around 15°C in the winter.

Succulents stretch out when they don't get enough sunlight. A lack of sunlight also tends to make the plant grow faster. You will first notice the succulent starting to turn and bend towards the light source. As it continues to grow, it will get taller, with more space between the leaves. Most of the time the leaves will become smaller and the colour will lose its intensity – which is particularly disappointing if you have purchased a purple, pink or red Echeveria!

Generally, you want your succulents to get as much indirect sunlight as possible. Especially in dark winters, it is almost impossible to grow them without some stretching. You could use a grow light to give your plants more light; there are lots of options on the market, like the stylish lights from Bulbo.

DID YOU KNOW

that the pearls of a String of Pearls plant are actually its leaves? Just like any succulent, they store water in their leaves, but these happen to look particularly cute. And while the leaves look delicious, like peas, they are somewhat poisonous to humans and animals. Make sure to hang them out of reach of children and pets.

CARE TIPS:

☀ *Location: Sunlight. The more colourful your succulent (purple, pink, red), the more direct sunlight is needed. Keep in bright indirect sunlight in the peak of summer to prevent sunburn.*

🌡 *Temperature: Room temperature. Succulents can tolerate dry air. To stimulate blooming, keep them at 10°C for a few weeks in the winter/very early spring.*

💧 *Watering: Better to underwater than over-water. Use well-draining soil (preferably succulent/cactus soil; with regular soil you'll need to mix something light and porous in to increase the drainage). Soak the soil when it's completely dry. Never water into the rosette.*

♡ *Fertilizer: Not needed. If you like, you can fertilize every 15 days during the growth period.*

GROW YOUR OWN SUCCULENTS

The most fun part of succulents: you can easily multiply your plants into a large family of succulents, because they are particularly easy to propagate. How?

∨ *Succulents like the jade plant, (Crassula ovata, bottom) can be easily propagated by placing a little cutting directly onto the soil. Water sparsely until the leaf sprouts roots.*

DO IT YOURSELF

(1) Gently pull a few leaves off from the stem of the plant (don't cut the leaves). If they don't come off, it helps to twist them a little bit. But be careful: it's important to have a clean pull, which means that nothing remains on the stem.

(2) Lay your fresh leaves horizontally on some soil. You can use a plate with a thin layer of soil or lay them at the foot of a plant in a pot. Now let your leaves dry out for a few days – don't water them immediately. After a few days gently sprinkle water over the leaves. Water again once the soil is completely dry. You can water once every 10 days or less. Like a grown-up succulent, they don't need a lot of water. Place your leaves in a place with lots of indirect sunlight.

(3) After a few weeks, some miniature white or pink roots will sprout from the tip of your leaves. And a teeny-tiny baby plant will start to grow. Once your new succulents are a little bit bigger, you'll notice that the initial leaves will become wrinkly, yellow or dry. You can carefully pull them off and plant the succulent in its own pot.

ALOE VERA

If you're looking for
one of the easiest houseplants ever,
opt for a beautiful aloe plant.

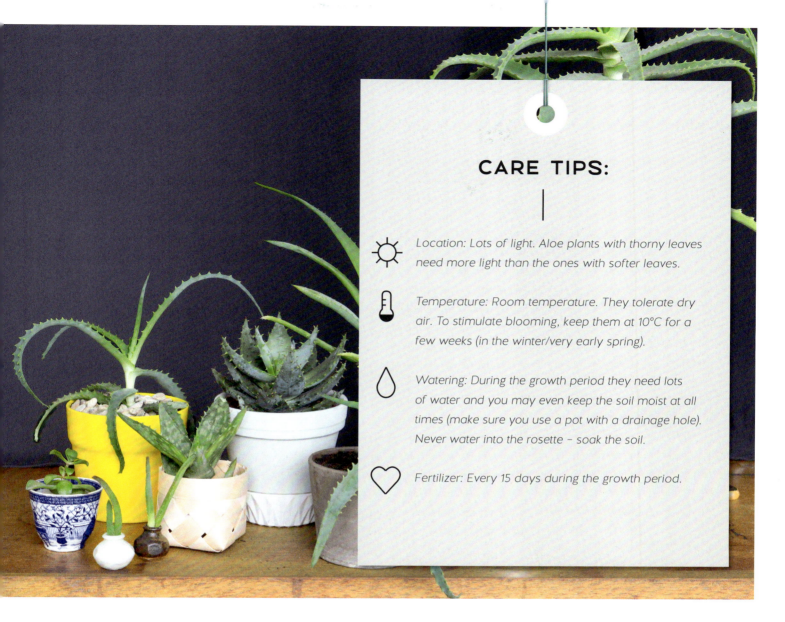

CARE TIPS:

Location: Lots of light. Aloe plants with thorny leaves need more light than the ones with softer leaves.

Temperature: Room temperature. They tolerate dry air. To stimulate blooming, keep them at 10°C for a few weeks (in the winter/very early spring).

Watering: During the growth period they need lots of water and you may even keep the soil moist at all times (make sure you use a pot with a drainage hole). Never water into the rosette – soak the soil.

Fertilizer: Every 15 days during the growth period.

The Ancient Greeks and Romans used aloe vera to treat wounds. In the Middle Ages, the yellowish liquid found inside the leaves was favoured as a purgative. As a herbal medicine, aloe vera juice is still commonly used internally to relieve digestive discomfort.

To use the gel of your own aloe, simply cut off a leaf. You will see that, depending on the thickness of the leaf, there is a translucent gel inside. You can rub it on your skin to relieve burns from the sun or the oven.

Aloe vera plants auto-propagate and grow new offshoots. When these are big enough, you can gently remove them from their mother plant in the early summer (including as much of the roots from the offshoot as possible) and plant them in a well-drained pot placed in bright indirect sunlight.

DID YOU KNOW

that it's not easy to make your aloe vera bloom indoors? Only mature plants (at least 4 years old) bloom, so don't expect too much from a small aloe vera plant. Give the plant as much direct sunlight as possible and some extra fertilizer every two weeks. Also remove all babies so it has more energy to put into producing beautiful flowers. If your aloe vera still won't bloom, simply enjoy the beauty and virtues of its leaves!

CACTI & SUCCULENTS

STYLING TIPS

Cacti and succulents are not only ideal beginner plants, but they also add a distinctive desert touch to a home. Whether you go for a giant specimen that looks like a true sculpture, or opt for a group of smaller cacti and succulents, the styling opportunities are endless. The secret to a great cactus styling is combining different kinds of textures: a cactus with big spines next to a hairy Old Man cactus? Why not!

∨ Create a little desert composition by placing different varieties of cacti and a Haworthia succulent in a glass bowl with some chunky pebbles. The wall decoration just got some serious spiky competition!

GENTLY WRAP
MAGAZINE PAPER AROUND
YOUR CACTUS WHEN
REPOTTING. IF YOU DON'T...
YOU MAY NEED TO USE
YOUR TWEEZERS.
OUCH!

STYLING TIP

Because most cactus plants grow upwards,
their plant pot is very much exposed.
This calls for creative pots that fit your interior style.
You can paint some simple terracotta pots, buy more
funky pots in a shop or make something yourself.
Do make sure the pots have an appropriate
drainage hole, because you don't want to kill
your spiky friends.

⌐ *Emphasize the large number of cactus*
varieties by showing them in a wooden cabinet.
∧ *The ideal location for cacti is on a sunny*
windowsill. Place them in a wooden crate so
that you can easily move them if you want
to water them or open the windows.

COOL IDEA

Cactus plants look best when they are paired with different kinds of cacti and other species. If you want to keep your #plantgang cactus-only, opt for any kind of Rhipsalis, also known as mistletoe cactus. Most Rhipsalis droop, but some are upright or sprawling. They add a different cactus texture to your cactus mix!

∧ *Add that little "je ne sais quoi": combine cacti with vintage treasures for a unique styling.*
> *A small cactus plant complements any styling.*

THE KEY TO HAPPILY
GROWING CACTI IS NOT
TO AVOID WATERING BUT
TO NOT OVERWATER
THEM.

∧ *Desert oasis perfectly interpreted: this
reading nook has an Arizona vibe!*

∧ *Plants & piano: a combination that makes our heart sing!*

A DARK WALL HELPS THE
VIBRANT GREEN OF
CACTI AND SUCCULENTS TO
"POP" - AND IS ALSO A
PERFECT BACKDROP FOR THE
SCULPTURAL SHAPES OF
THE PLANTS.

STYLING TIP

*If you want to decorate your piano with plants,
use pots without drainage holes to avoid water
stains or spilling. Make sure you put clay drainage
balls at the bottom of your pots and use
succulent or cactus soil.*

⌐ *A cosy nook with a big aloe vera and stylish
accessories.*
∧ *Succulent leaves are delicate as glass and stain
slightly when you touch them.*

CACTI AND SUCCULENTS
ARE LIKE LIVING
SCULPTURES. THEY CAN
BE THE HIGHLIGHT
OF ANY ROOM.

< *A big Euphorbia triangula is a statement piece in this room. The watering can on the sideboard blends right in.*

∟ *A bookcase decorated with an eclectic mix of African art, design classics, books, pretty boxes and plants in different sizes.*

∨ *Sunny bedrooms are the ideal place for a big ornamental succulent. Sleeping next to your favourite green buddy is the best!*

JESKA & DEAN

Hastings / England

GREEN GEM ON THE ENGLISH CHANNEL

You won't find a TV here. Or any glossy new furniture pieces, for that matter. Jeska and Dean Hearne's little
bungalow close to Hastings in England can truly be called a collected home, brimming with character
and personality. It has been created over time with lots of love, creativity and warmth, and is home not only to
the two young creatives, but to their two cats, Marlo and Wallis, and around 60 plants.

∨ Happiness on the doorstep of creative couple Jeska and Dean's house, where they live with their cats Wallis and Marlo.

Perched on the chalky cliffs of the English Channel, the home speaks visually about its owners: Jeska works as a blogger, stylist and photographer and runs her own online shop, "The Future Kept". Dean freelances as a graphic designer, web designer and photographer, while also collaborating with Jeska on the online shop.

Since 2013 Jeska and Dean have lived in the bungalow with a large, wild backyard. The creative couple constantly change and rearrange the house, which is home and workplace for them both. What first strikes you upon entering the cosy home is the concept and attitude of life that Jeska and Dean share. Their sustainable way of life is obvious: vintage furniture is paired with flea market finds; earthy hues dominate; thoughtfully collected and displayed ceramics stand side by side with a lush bunch of houseplants. Jeska has a wide array of happy and healthy plants – from small succulents and thriving ferns to leafy Monstera, Ficus elastica and Calathea orbifolia.

∧ *The antique Victorian glass cabinet in the workspace offers unique opportunities to decorate. Paired with a classic crawling ivy vine.*

> *In the workspace, Jeska and Dean prepare orders for their clients. The high shelf keeps plants, magazines, wrapping tools and ribbons safe from curious cats.*

MY FAVOURITE PLANT IS A TRADESCANTIA
ZEBRINA THAT MY FRIEND SARAH-LOU GAVE ME LAST
YEAR. IT WAS A SMALL CUTTING THAT HAS FLOURISHED
INTO A TRAILING BEAUTY, AND IT ALWAYS MAKES ME
SMILE WHEN I SEE IT AND THINK OF MY FRIEND.
A PLANT IS SUCH A THOUGHTFUL GIFT.

SEE PAGE 120

∨ *A young Monstera deliciosa has its own corner in the couple's bedroom.*

SEE PAGE 60

⌐ *Jeska's nightstand is home to a vase terrarium (see instructions on page 57), a Haworthia, her favorite scented candle, a chocolate bar and vintage frames.*
∧ *A Senecio kleiniiformis looks elegant in a vintage brass pot.*

∧ *A little piece of the seaside in the bathroom with a palm, a string of pearls plant, a flowering geranium, a trailing fern and big shells.*

Despite the large number of plants, the bungalow does not feel overwhelming or crowded. With the skilful eye of a stylist, Jeska has managed to include plants in every room without compromising on airiness and free space.

The plant stylings are simple and refined at the same time: slick ensembles encompass ferns and a trio of vintage vases, tropical plants are matched with a portrait of a Polynesian woman, and a large Stephanotis plant has stretched its green shoots behind a comfy vintage chair. The styling secret seems obvious: plant stylings have the best effect when they're formed around a certain theme and enriched with appropriate décor items. Bigger houseplants, however, like to perform as solo artists, claiming their space and providing striking visual effects.

Jeska's creativity combined with Dean's handy craftsman skills are a perfect starting point for simple yet unique DIY ideas with plants. Jeska has created a little terrarium without investing in a pricey

∧ The deep dark green of the *Fatsia japonica* plant is complemented by the deep charcoal wall. Vintage prints and artwork, and a very old mirror, add boho charm to this part of the living room.

CALATHEA ORBIFOLIA
IS NATIVE TO BOLIVIA. THE
BEAUTIFUL PATTERN OF THE
LARGE LEAVES MAKES IT A
STYLING FAVOURITE.

THE RUSTIC VINTAGE
TERRACOTTA POTS
WERE A HAPPY FIND.
AMAZINGLY, THEY WERE
IN THE OLD SHED
WHEN WE MOVED IN.

COOL IDEA

Never throw away old pallets and crates. The wood has a lovely patina that gives instant charm to the new things you can create with it. Dean made this small wooden cabinet by hand from some old palettes – it is now home to some parsley and basil, an ivy vine and a flowering Haworthia.

terrarium vessel or special equipment. A large glass vase, some pebbles and a constant sprinkling with water provide a perfect micro cosmos for a humidity-loving plant. What's more, it looks utterly stylish on her bedside table and completes the earthy vintage look.

The DIY kitchen shelf is yet another of Jeska and Dean's ideas. While working on another project, they came up with the idea of upcycling some old pallets and creating a simple, rustic shelving unit for the kitchen wall. Jeska had a clear image in mind: something with a patina and enough space for her favourite herbs, like basil, mint and coriander, as well as some additional kitchenware and more plants. On the other side of the kitchen, the long windowsill hosts a full line-up of smaller cacti, succulents and cuttings in various vintage glasses. A visual treat while cooking!

Their cats, Wallis and Marlo, are not too impressed by the sweet scent of baked cinnamon rolls and freshly brewed coffee – they take their inspection rounds seriously, and prefer to nibble on some plants instead. The harmony of cohabitation, where everyone has room to follow their instincts and live creatively, is so typical of this home.

EVERYTHING IN OUR HOME HAS A MEANING AND WAS CAREFULLY COLLECTED. IT'S AN EXPRESSION OF OUR PERSONALITY.

< *Cat Wallis loves to snuggle in the cosy living room – and sometimes to nibble on the plants.*
> *A tiny Senecio rowleyanus cutting growing on the windowsill.*

<Cat Wallis on a treasure hunt.
∨ A small Ficus elastica, ceramics from their own store
and some bottles on top of the vintage chest of drawers.

The little home of Jeska and Dean Hearne is a warm and cosy nest atop the English cliffs, filled with personality and creativity. It speaks about its owners and reveals their unique characters and their understanding of a simple yet confident life. Being surrounded by plants is the most natural way of life for both of them, but it's also more than that. Living with nature – indoors and outdoors – combining vintage and handmade, working and relaxing in the same space: everything seems to be in a healthy and aesthetic balance here. For Jeska, Dean, Wallis and Marlo.

→ *Find out more about Jeska and Dean at TheFutureKept.com and lobsterandswan.com*

DID YOU KNOW

it's important to clean the leaves of your leafy plants like Calathea, Monstera deliciosa and Ficus elastica? When plants are coated with dust, the openings through which they exhale oxygen and inhale carbon dioxide become blocked and their air-purifying powers are drastically reduced. Don't try to make the leaves shine with oil – this will only attract more dust. Simply use a damp cloth and some mild soap.

CREATE YOUR OWN TERRARIUM

A simple version with no special equipment or purchased terrarium vessels.

1. *Pick a large glass vase with a wide opening, big enough to hold a terracotta pot.*

2. *Cover the bottom of the vase with small pebbles and sprinkle some water over them, so they are moist.*

3. *Delicately place a potted plant of your choice in the vase on top of the pebbles, being careful not to damage any leaves. Peperomia plants love the extra humidity inside a terrarium like this.*

4. *Mist or sprinkle the pebbles regularly, and water the plant as usual.*

∨ *The garden behind the house, on a breezy clifftop that has a sea view if you stand on your toes, is used for repotting and relaxing.*

5 QUESTIONS

FOR JESKA

1 What does living with plants mean to you?
After I learnt to keep my first few plants alive, being surrounded by them definitely evolved into a natural way of life for us. Both our parents have always had plants in their homes and love gardening too. I grew up in the late '70s and early '80s surrounded by huge cheese plants, bonsai trees and cacti. There was always an avocado pip suspended in a jar of water on our kitchen windowsill, too, that my dad was trying to germinate. I loved visiting my neighbours' greenhouse as a child, and my grandma has a floral jungle in her conservatory, so I think it was always in the stars that I would be a plant keeper.

2 What do you value about your plants?
I can't imagine not being surrounded by green things. They make the air cleaner and our home a happier place to be. Spending some time each week tending to them is the closest thing to meditation for me. It makes me feel calm and happy.

3 Plant care seems daunting to some people. How do you care for your plants? What is your routine, if any?
I will admit that I am loving but a bit haphazard with my plant care. I have kept most alive with just watering little and often, a "treat them mean – keep them keen" approach. I feed them in growing season when I remember, and of course I do talk to them too. ;)

4 Do you have a secret plant-care tip to share?
Don't be scared of experimenting with cuttings – you always learn more each time you try. A few might die, but lots will survive and you can nurture them into fully grown plants.

5 Plants are a wonderful addition to any interior. What is your styling tip when it comes to plants?
Gather them in little groups of different leaf shapes and colours – mix their textures, pair feathery ferns with tough full-leaved plants. Just generally go wild with layering different pots, heights and so on.

STYLING TIP

Look for old terracotta pots at flea markets, farmer's markets, garage sales or second-hand shops. Or create that rugged look yourself by painting your new terracotta pots with garden lime. Sand them afterwards for a more "used" look.

MONSTERA DELICIOSA

PLANT PORTRAIT

SWISS CHEESE PLANT

With its lush, wild appearance, large split leaves and swinging aerial roots, the Monstera deliciosa is a real jungle queen. If you aim for an instant jungle look in your home, this is the plant to go for. Unlike many other plants, the Monstera deliciosa guarantees an instant jungle vibe in any room. And yet this spectacular houseplant is very easy-going. The Swiss cheese plant is a low-maintenance houseplant and thus ideal for anyone who considers themselves to have a black thumb.

The Monstera deliciosa is an evergreen epiphyte with aerial roots from the arum family Araceae and is native to Mexico and Central America. Taken out of her natural habitat, this species is also a favourite houseplant. As early as the 1960s and 1970s, the Swiss cheese plant accounted for real urban jungles throughout the interiors of everything from stylish designer homes to simple worker dwellings.

This low-maintenance houseplant features decorative heart-shaped leaves with holes (younger leaves have no holes) and small anchoring roots as well as long aerial roots. These long aerial roots are used to absorb important nutrients and water and should not be cut back. The lush leaves, however, can be pruned back if desired, and the cuttings can serve to propagate the plant. Simply put the cutting into fresh water and wait until the first white roots start growing. Afterwards, these cuttings can easily be potted into a new plant pot.

∧ *With its giant leaves and aerial roots, Monstera is not a plant for a small apartment but can add a real jungle vibe to your home. Especially when you pair it with other leafy fellows.*

DID YOU KNOW

that in its natural habitat Monstera deliciosa also grows edible fruit? In some countries Monstera deliciosa fruits are considered a rare and expensive delicacy. It is not a coincidence that it is called a Monstera deliciosa, or "fruit salad plant".

Due to its abundant growth and size this plant is a great solo performer in sunny or semi-shaded corners of your home. The Monstera deliciosa is great as a statement plant when it has enough room to grow and spread out. Support its upright growth by adding a climbing pole, and you will be rewarded with a real jungle look.

The Swiss cheese plant is a great option for any kind of interior style: it perfectly enriches monochromatic, Nordic interiors and contemporary homes, as well as eclectic and bohemian interiors. To accentuate your preferred style, choose suitable accessories to go with your Monstera plant.

⌐ *Monstera deliciosa is not a plant for your windowsill. It needs space and will roar for it should you not give some.*

∧ *If you don't like the classic moss poles, you can also opt for a sturdy, natural bamboo stick to support your Monstera.*

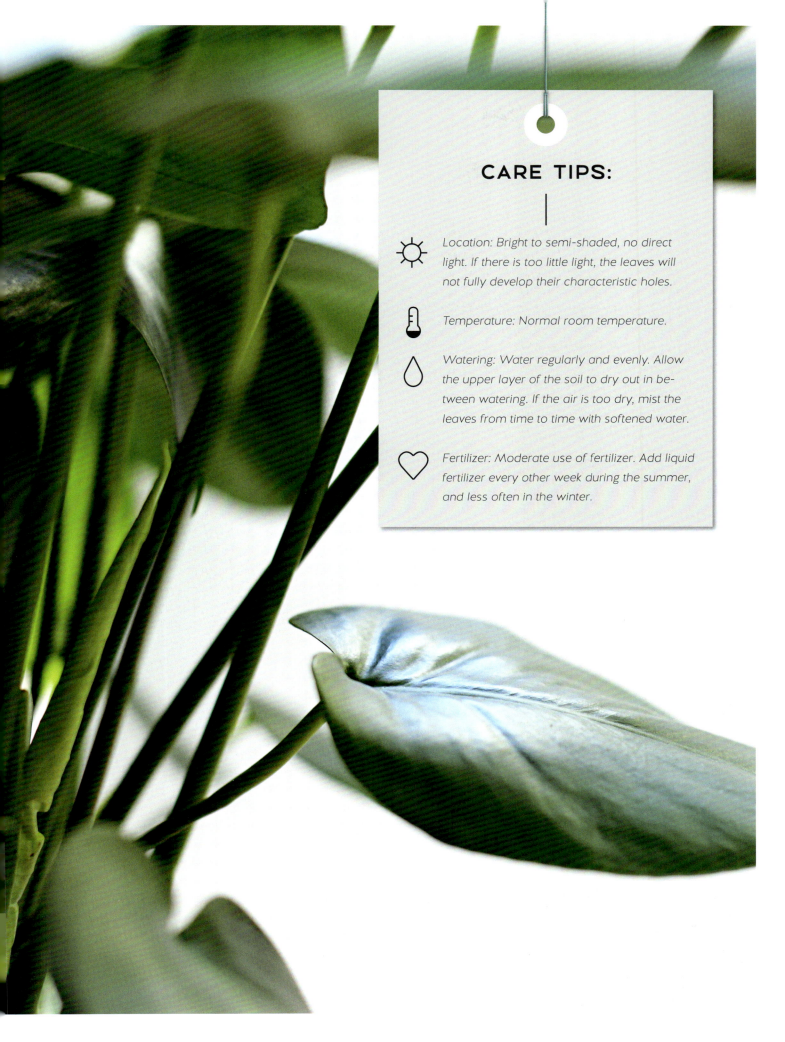

CARE TIPS:

Location: Bright to semi-shaded, no direct light. If there is too little light, the leaves will not fully develop their characteristic holes.

Temperature: Normal room temperature.

Watering: Water regularly and evenly. Allow the upper layer of the soil to dry out in between watering. If the air is too dry, mist the leaves from time to time with softened water.

Fertilizer: Moderate use of fertilizer. Add liquid fertilizer every other week during the summer, and less often in the winter.

OXALIS TRIANGULARIS

PURPLE SHAMROCK

If one could turn a swarm of purple butterflies into a plant, it would become an Oxalis triangularis. This beautiful houseplant for sunny windowsills belongs to the family of wood sorrels (Oxalidaceae) and is also known as the purple shamrock or love plant.

< If you forget to water your Oxalis or temperatures drop too low, everything above the surface will wilt and your plant will take refuge in the bulbs below.
∨ The edible flowers of the Oxalis triangularis are white lilac and add lots of charm to a summer salad!

This elegant beauty is not as delicate and subtle as one would expect: lots of sunlight, a little water and the Oxalis is happy. The plant is not hardy and should not overwinter outdoors, but otherwise it is relatively undemanding.

Not only does the Oxalis triangularis fascinate with its beautiful triangular leaves, but the plant also blooms regularly, presenting small white-pink or violet flowers on long stalks. In addition, the plant exists in two colour varieties: with violet leaves and white-pink flowers and with green leaves and white flowers. Both are real eye-catchers in the home. A very special feature of the Oxalis triangularis is that they close their leaves at night and open them again in the early morning. This gives the plant an extra little something.

DID YOU KNOW

that the love plant is also edible?
The leaves and flowers can be
eaten raw or cooked and have a fruity,
sour taste. Oxalis flowers and leaves are
a delicious and very decorative addition
to a salad. Due to the oxalic acid
contained in the plant, you should not
eat the entire plant, though:
this could lead to digestive problems.
And important for cat owners:
the Oxalis triangularis is toxic to cats.

SEE PAGE 22

AT NIGHT THE OXALIS
GOES TO SLEEP. IT FOLDS
ITS LEAVES BACK LIKE AN
UMBRELLA AND ARISES
FROM ITS NIGHT OF SLEEP
IN THE MORNING.

CARE TIPS:

Location: Very bright, but no direct sunlight. The ideal location has morning or evening sunshine. Perfect for the windowsill.

Temperature: Normal room temperature. The plant cannot tolerate frost.

Watering: Water regularly, but only when the top layer of soil is dry. Avoid waterlogging, because the plant does not tolerate it. Water sparsely in the winter, unless the plant is kept in a heated (and thus dry) room.

Fertilizer: In the summer, add some liquid fertilizer once a month.

MONSTERA DELICIOSA

The queen of the jungle is very much back in style. The Swiss cheese plant was a popular houseplant in the 1960s and 1970s. Today, the Monstera has shed its outdated image for good and embellishes homes around the world. It is an all-round styling champion and fits into the most pure Scandi interiors as well colourful boho homes.

∨ *Monstera deliciosa is a climbing plant that uses its aerial roots as vertical supports. Give your Monstera a moss pole to prevent the plant from bending over, which can be damaging to the stems.*

AS MONSTERA DELICIOSA GROWS OLDER, ITS LEAVES WILL GET BIGGER AND THEY WILL DEVELOP MORE HOLES.

STYLING TIP

By simply changing the planter of your Monstera deliciosa, you can make it part of your interior style. Cool monochrome pots fit in Scandinavian interiors, and simple terracotta pots or woven baskets fit nicely into a home with a natural or boho look. If the Monstera is not yet fully grown, it can be placed on a stool: a proper throne for the queen of the jungle.

⌐ *For a graphic touch, place your Monstera in black and white wire baskets.*

∧ *A Monstera deliciosa becomes a jungalicious eye-catcher when you place it on a simple stool.*

PEPPER, MICHAEL & NAHELE

Mühlhausen / Germany

GREENER LIVING NEAR HEIDELBERG

Style resides in this home. This is obvious from the very first moment you cross the threshold of the Schmidt family's house. The young family consists of mum Pepper, dad Michael and two-year-old Nahele, fondly called "Waldmöwe", which is a literal German translation of her Hawaiian name.

∧ *This is what slow family living looks like: the cute little Schmidt family, surrounded by plants.*

< *The vintage cabinet houses snail shells, stones, shells and a wonderful collection of air plants (Tillandsia).*

∨ *Two Echeveria are cosied up in an old coffee grinder. Line the drawer with cling film to protect it from moisture.*

Pepper, Michael and Nahele's semi-detached house is located a 30-minute drive south of the German city of Heidelberg and is inhabited not only by the happy family but by a big bunch of cuddly toys and plants as well.

"A room without plants appears shallow, almost dead." Pepper kicks off our plant conversation with a strong and comprehensible opinion. And she lives by her words – plants thrive on all three floors and in all rooms of the house: in the kitchen, the bedroom, Nahele's room and the bathroom. Plants are also essential for Pepper's style philosophy. She has named her own style "Scethno": a mix of Scandinavian clear lines and neutral colours combined with wild, primal patterns of an ethno style and collectibles from Africa. All of this is brought to perfection by the addition of a growing houseplant collection.

DID YOU KNOW

Tillandsia use their specialized leaves to absorb water and nutrients from the air, which is why they are known as air plants? Most Tillandsias come from humid climates, so they appreciate high levels of humidity. Placing them next to potted plants will be a great help to them since they will be able to absorb the moisture that evaporates off the other plants when they're watered.

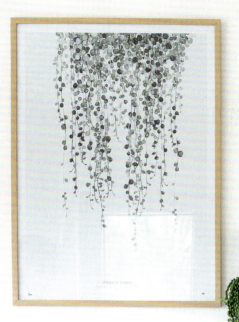

∧ You can turn an empty corner with only four plants into a botanical gallery by adding plant-inspired artwork. The framed leaves, leaf prints and posters are by Maaike Koster from My Deer Art Shop (mydeerartshop.nl).

SEE PAGE 60

The paper bag®

This bag is made from organic paper.
It is 100% natural.
180 g/m² double-layer paper:
white kraft layered with brown kraft.
Capacity: 33 litres.
100% Ecographik™
Do not throw it away.
It is reusable.

ᴠ *Chlorophytum comosum, more commonly known as the spider plant, is one of the easiest houseplants out there, suited for every room in the house, including the bathroom. When happy with their conditions, spider plants start growing little babies that you can replant and share with family or friends.*

AS A GIRL SCOUT I ALWAYS LOVED BEING OUTDOORS. BECAUSE NATURE AT HOME IS VERY IMPORTANT TO ME, PLANTS ARE INDISPENSABLE.

The line between nature and living space is fluid at the Schmidts'. The green outdoor surroundings seem to blend with the indoor plants, thanks to numerous large windows and open fronts. The Hoya is a special plant mate of Pepper – she has a large variety of Hoya plants throughout her home and admits that these wax plants are her favourites. This species is of tropical origin, stemming from Asia, Australia and Polynesia, and is renowned for its beautiful, waxy blooms. Pepper prefers to keep her Hoyas as trailing plants instead of supporting an upward growth. The Hoya carnosa is one of the most common houseplants of this species and it thrives in Pepper's kitchen and Nahele's room. Moreover, she also owns some Hoya obovata and kerrii, as well as a number of "string of pearls" plants. These stand side by side with cheerful Pilea peperomioides plants and quite a few bonsai trees throughout the home.

A great deal of furniture pieces and décor items are vintage finds from various online platforms. Pepper even sources plants on-line; most of them are second-hand and come from owners who have no space for them anymore or simply want to get rid of them. Often these plant treasures turn out to be located in the neighbour-hood – one of those happy finds is her almost two-metre tall Ficus elastica that outgrew his previous home and now thrives in Pepper's living room, entangled with a Ceropegia plant.

You might think that someone who owns so many plants would lose track of ideal plant care. But Pepper has found her own way of keeping up with her plants and plant-care instructions: she keeps a "Jungle Book", a sort of plant diary with handy plant-care tips and the botanical names of her plants. She takes notes about how her plants feel in certain spots in the home and when she moves them to another area. She also sticks to a certain day in the week for plant care – with these simple tricks plant care is much more efficient and definitely easier.

But it's not only the fine selection of plants that strikes the beholder's eye in this light-filled home. Pepper's apt styling skills render simple plants into decorative vignettes throughout the house. Her ideas –

↗ *Not only does the Tropaeolum (nasturtium) look elegant, but it's also edible and grows delicious orange or yellow flowers that make every salad look great.*

> *Pepper obtained this old display cabinet from a zoo. Today, it serves as a greenhouse in the bedroom.*

∨ Pepper's collection of wooden bowls, earthenware and ceramic, with a trailing Hoya at the top.

SECOND-HAND PLANTS ARE A GREAT ALTERNATIVE TO CONVENTIONAL PLANTS FROM GARDEN CENTRES. CHECK PORTALS SUCH AS EBAY FOR PLANTS – SOMETIMES YOU CAN FIND REAL GREEN GEMS ONLINE.

DID YOU KNOW

that Hoya carnosa grows beautiful flowers in the summer? They are sweetly scented and look like little bouquets of starry flowers. Make sure not to move the plant when it's blooming, as it will cause it to lose its flowers.

like the vintage wooden display case in the dining area, featuring a variety of air plants – are impeccably executed and wittily interpreted. Another Tillandsia is fixed with wire on a wooden base and serves as a centrepiece on the table, while driftwood from a nearby river is transformed into hangers for kitchenware and plants. And speaking of wit: how about some small succulents in a vintage coffee grinder? We say yes!

In her home office, Pepper uses a simple styling trick to highlight the botanical beauty: she pairs real plants with their illustrated counterparts on beautiful posters from the Dutch label My Deer Art. To break up the style, she adds her own botanical frames

∨ Pepper's talent for DIY is visible in her kitchen: a hanger for dish towels and plants was made of leather straps and a piece of driftwood. The leather drawer pulls are also her work.

with dried leaves. The entire look has a striking effect, mixing depth, textures and sizes. Another favourite prop for plant stylings are woven baskets with ethnic patterns – Pepper uses these to cover up unspectacular plant pots and thus adds a bohemian vibe to her houseplants.

The family's affinity to nature is evident throughout the entire home. But the exterior is equally important for the Schmidts. A spacious terrace is an area to relax and spend time with family and friends, and it also provides the setting for Pepper's gardening projects. The adjacent garden with tall trees – a favourite playground for Nahele – perfectly connects the home with the surrounding nature.

The home of the Schmidt family is a wonderful example that living with a lively toddler does not have to mean abstaining from plants. Combining family life, happy plants and an impeccable interior style works well – given some styling skills, lots of love and a happy family spirit.

CARE TIP

A plant journal is very helpful. I stick the original plant tags inside and note how plants react to a specific spot, as well as problems that arise and what helped to overcome them. I also collect plant-care tips that I find online.

⌐ *The blackboard wall in the nursery is a cool background for the plants and a creative canvas for Nahele.*

> *Pepper keeps a plant diary in which she gathers plant-care tips and tricks.*

I ALWAYS TAKE CARE OF
THE PLANTS AFTER NAHELE'S
SUNDAY BATH, SO THAT I
CAN USE THE WATER FOR
THE PLANTS.

Λ *Even the child's room is decorated with small, non-poisonous plants like cacti (which are out of reach) and Hoyas.*

∨ In nature, rubber plants can grow up to 30 metres high, but you can keep them from growing too tall by pruning the top.

> Superwoman styling: a bonsai, a Hoya, driftwood, books, magazines and a small wooden kiwi make a typical "Scethno" still life.

SEE PAGE 88

A FEW APTLY PLACED PLANTS ENLIVEN EVEN A MINIMALISTIC STYLING.

∨ *Life's simple pleasures: creating family art at the dinner table, surrounded by plants.*

5 QUESTIONS
FOR PEPPER

1 **Living with plants – what does it mean to you?**
Above all, it means that nature does not begin at my doorstep. I like keeping the line between home and nature rather blurry.

2 **Your home is very stylish. How would you describe your interior style?**
I define my style with the self-chosen term "Scethno" – it combines the purity of Scandinavian shapes and colours with primal ethnic patterns and collectibles from Africa. I like the Nordic reservedness, but only when it is contrasted with material structures and history. I like to be surrounded by things in my home that tell a story – be it our own travel mementos or the life story of complete strangers.

3 **When choosing new plants for your home, do you pick them with the eye of an interior expert, or is your choice rather based on emotional impulse?**
Either way. I choose most of my plants from a visual point of view, because of their appearance. Often, I know in advance what kind of styling I want to achieve with them. But sometimes I end up buying plants spontaneously in a garden centre just because they happened to catch my eye.

4 **Do you have a favourite houseplant? If so, which one and why?**
I do have a few, actually. I like the Hoya obovata and kerrii because of their succulent, unusual leaves. On the other hand, I also like the string of pearls plant and the Pilea peperomioides, because they look wonderful in pictures, and bonsai are dear to me because they are actual trees and look utterly elegant.

5 **Do you have any further plants on your wish list?**
Yes, a few. I'd love to get a really big olive tree, a bonsai that looks like the famous Hometree in the movie Avatar and a tall Hoya kerrii.

STYLING TIP

Plants that are not too compact work best. I make sure that the plants that I use have interesting shapes and leaves and an overall airy appearance. Like the Hoya, for example, which I prefer as a trailing plant rather than attached to a trellis. Bonsai are great solo players – they don't need much additional decoration. In general, it's important to stick to a colour palette to create a well-balanced look. For me that means that I only have green plants: no bicoloured or tricoloured plants, and no flowering or red-leaved ones either.

PLANT STANDS IN WOOD AND COPPER

Blogger Antonia from Craftifair shows how you can easily create these stylish plant stands, which will raise your jungle plants in style.

^ The Zamioculcas zamiifolia, also known as the ZZ plant, is a sturdy plant with shiny green leaves. The leaves have a regular pattern and perfectly accentuate the style of the DIY plant stand.

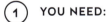
YOU NEED:

• Four round dowel rods with a diameter of 18 or 22 mm and length of 1 metre (from the hardware store)
• Six T-connections of copper pipe with an inside diameter of 18 or 22 mm (from the plumbing department at the hardware store)
• Ruler, pencil and jigsaw

② To create the legs, mark on the dowel rods where to saw them. If you want your plant stand to be around 50 cm tall, saw four rods of 40 cm and four sticks of 10 cm. The longer the legs (and the larger the space in the middle), the more unstable your plant stand will be. A long and a short stick together make one plant stand leg.

③ The cross for the centrepiece is made with five pieces of wood and two copper T-connections. The length of the individual wooden sticks will be determined by the size of your plant pot.

④ Smooth the ends of the wooden dowel rods with sandpaper. As the last step, attach the legs to the centrepiece.

→ Find out more about this and other projects at craftifair.com

FICUS ELASTICA

RUBBER TREE PLANT

A Ficus elastica has many benefits. Besides its handsome dark and glossy look, it's also particularly effective at removing formaldehyde from the air. It's one of the more powerful air-purifying plants out there.

< *Meet Marvin (as in Gaye): this tall rubber plant watches over the entire plantgang, gracefully displayed on and around an old folding ladder.*
∨ *Usually Marvin hangs out in the dining area.*

Ficus elastica, commonly known as rubber plant, is native to northeast India, Nepal, Bhutan, Burma, China, Malaysia and Indonesia. In its natural habitat, it grows over 30 metres tall. Indoor plants have a more manageable height, however: between two and three metres. Once the rubber plant has grown to the desired height, you can cut the top off. You may also want to prune back any unwanted branches to give the plant a fuller shape. It's best to prune in spring or summer, but any other time is also fine. Just like many other plants in the fig family, a Ficus elastica doesn't like to be moved around. Treat it gently: sudden changes in temperature and light may cause it to drop its leaves.

Ficus is Latin for "fig", and like all figs, the ficus elastica contains a milky white latex, a chemical compound which is separate from its sap and is carried and stored in different cells. In the past, this latex was used to make rubber, but the rubber in Hevea

DID YOU KNOW

that in India there are "living bridges" grown with the roots of the Ficus elastica? A Ficus is planted on both sides of a river, and the roots are then guided with a hollow tree trunk (which rots away with time). After ten to fifteen years the roots are strong enough for people to walk across to the other side!

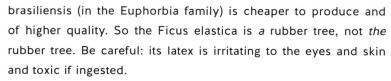

∧ *A dark green smaller-scale rubber tree on this sideboard. The rubber tree adds height and gloss to this group of plants.*

DID YOU KNOW

that the rubber tree is a perfect solo artist that also works great in groups? Tall, mature plants upgrade any corner. Mix and match it with palm trees, Sansevieria and colourful Calathea for an inspiring boho look. Add textiles with ethnic patterns, like kilim rugs and pillows, some leather poufs and a pile of books, and you immediately have a cosy reading nook. Ficus elastica also shines in monochrome and Scandinavian interiors. Use one plant as a living sculpture with lots of white and wood.

∧ *A smaller Ficus elastica can grow in a regular terracotta pot and looks great paired with other houseplants on a windowsill.*

brasiliensis (in the Euphorbia family) is cheaper to produce and of higher quality. So the Ficus elastica is *a* rubber tree, not *the* rubber tree. Be careful: its latex is irritating to the eyes and skin and toxic if ingested.

The rubber tree plant's deep green glossy leaves are a particularly beautiful feature. These tend to attract quite some dust, so to keep the leaves of your tree looking shiny and glossy, gently wipe them with a very soft cloth or sponge and lukewarm water.

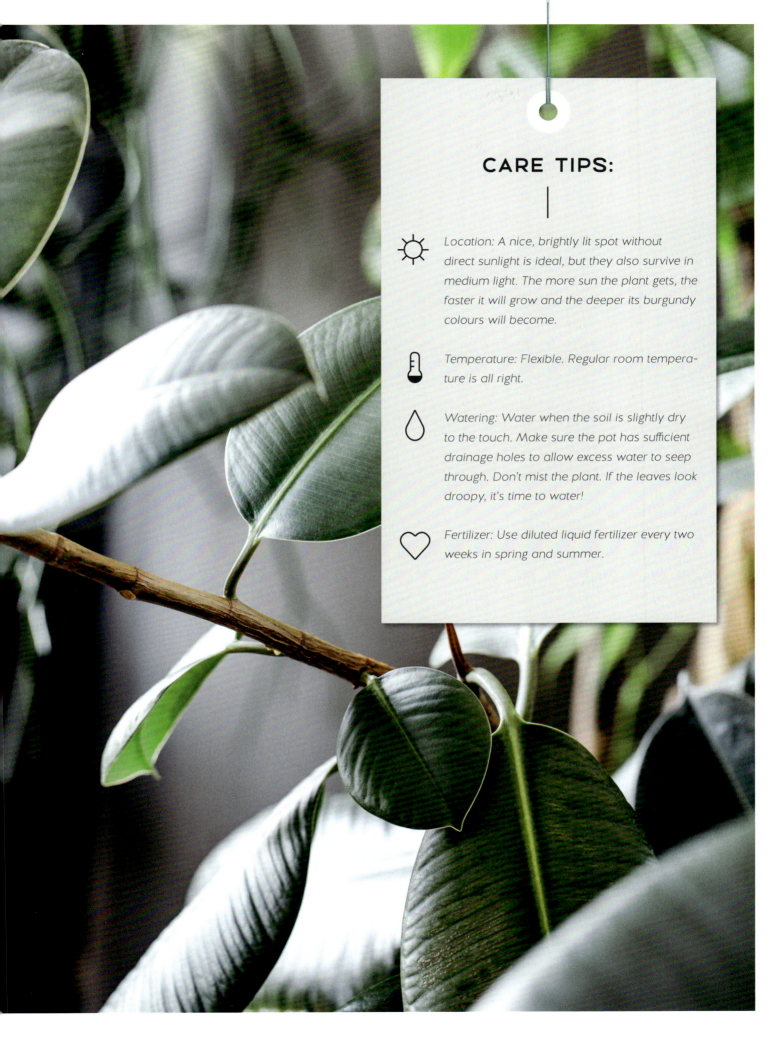

CARE TIPS:

☀ *Location: A nice, brightly lit spot without direct sunlight is ideal, but they also survive in medium light. The more sun the plant gets, the faster it will grow and the deeper its burgundy colours will become.*

🌡 *Temperature: Flexible. Regular room temperature is all right.*

💧 *Watering: Water when the soil is slightly dry to the touch. Make sure the pot has sufficient drainage holes to allow excess water to seep through. Don't mist the plant. If the leaves look droopy, it's time to water!*

♡ *Fertilizer: Use diluted liquid fertilizer every two weeks in spring and summer.*

CALATHEA

PRAYER PLANT

If you're looking for an instant leafy jungle feeling in your home, get yourself a Calathea.
This beautiful, lush plant stems from the Amazon jungle and comes with a fascinating array of leaves,
whose remarkable patterns make the Calathea very decorative

Calathea come in many different colours and patterns, from fresh green to deep purple and patterned leaves. The underside of the leaves is burgundy. But this wonderful houseplant is more than a great decorative element for your home: the wild jungle beauty is also a natural air purifier and reduces stress levels, making it beneficial for a healthy living environment. These facts make the Calathea the perfect green roommate.

Another special feature is Calathea's daily habit of folding and unfolding their leaves. This is why they are called prayer plants: every night their leaves fold together upwards, mimicking human hands folded in prayer. In the morning, they unfold themselves into their full glorious beauty again, so that they are able to soak up as much sunlight as possible.

In its natural habitat, the Calathea dwells in forest areas shaded by trees without direct sunlight, which is why a bright but

DID YOU KNOW

that the pattern on the Calathea lancifolia (see photo on page 10) actually looks like many smaller leaves? This makes the plant less interesting for herbivores to eat, because they tend to prefer large leaves. Calathea are smart like that!

∨ *Altitude games: Plants placed at different heights are great eye-catchers. The bushy Calathea, however, is perfectly remarkable on the floor by itself.*

semi-shaded spot within a warm home suits it very well. To keep your Calathea happy and healthy, it's important to mist the leaves and keep the soil moist at all times. Provide humid air if possible. In our heated apartments it can be difficult to maintain high humidity throughout the year. Using a humidity tray or electronic humidifier can help, but simply placing your Calathea together with other plants will also improve humidity. Who can resist a thriving #plantgang anyway?!

If your Calathea is not getting enough water or humidity, it will let you know! Its leaves will start to curl, the leaf tips will become brown or the leaves will simply fall off. Mist your plant a bit more often and give it some more water, and your Calathea will be back to its beautiful self in no time.

Because Calathea thrive in semi-shaded to shaded areas, they are the perfect plant for a hallway, bathroom or bedroom with less light. Although you may want to make sure you aren't surprised (or woken up!) by the sound of the folding movements in the evening or early morning.

BATHROOMS WITH NATURAL LIGHT ARE THE PERFECT SPOT FOR THE CALATHEA. THE WARM, HUMID AIR RESEMBLES THE PLANT'S TROPICAL HABITAT AND ENSURES HEALTHY GROWTH.

∧ *Calathea benefit from a group situation, where air humidity is slightly higher.*

∨ *A corner with indirect light is the perfect spot for a Calathea orbifolia.*

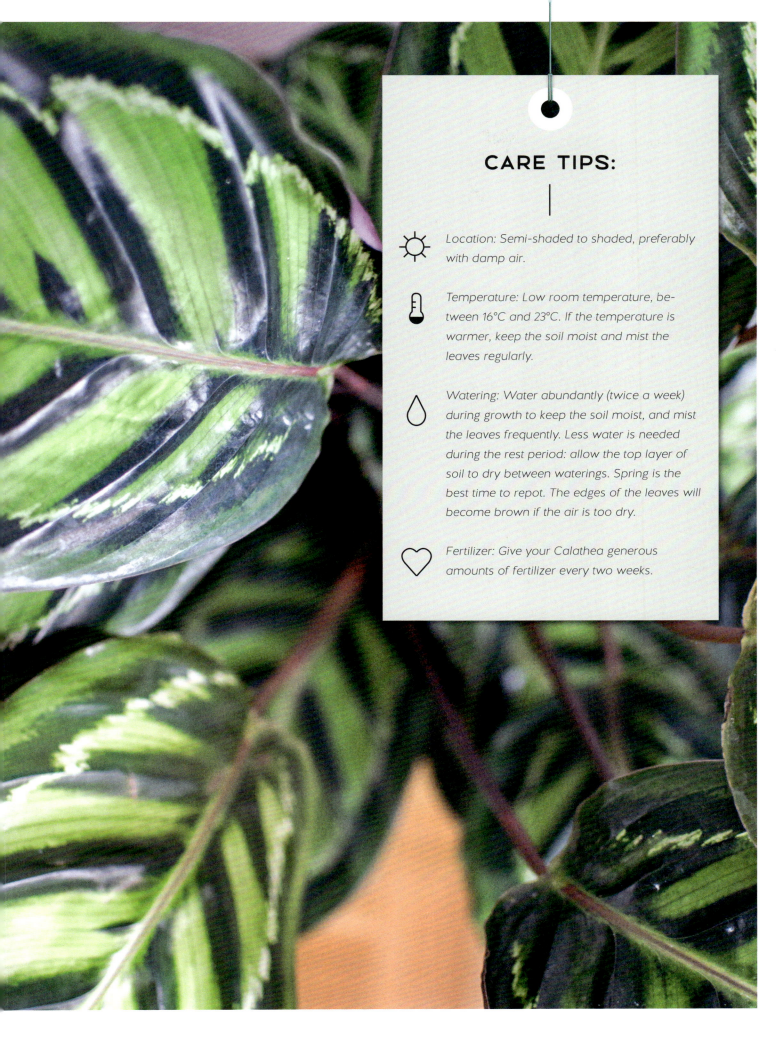

CARE TIPS:

Location: Semi-shaded to shaded, preferably with damp air.

Temperature: Low room temperature, between 16°C and 23°C. If the temperature is warmer, keep the soil moist and mist the leaves regularly.

Watering: Water abundantly (twice a week) during growth to keep the soil moist, and mist the leaves frequently. Less water is needed during the rest period: allow the top layer of soil to dry between waterings. Spring is the best time to repot. The edges of the leaves will become brown if the air is too dry.

Fertilizer: Give your Calathea generous amounts of fertilizer every two weeks.

FICUS ELASTICA & CALATHEA

STYLING TIPS

The rubber tree and the Calathea look good all alone or as part of a plantgang.
The Ficus elastica impresses with its size and often peculiar growth form, whereas the
Calathea scores with its remarkable leaf patterns and hues. If you opt for
single plants, choose more mature specimens. If you go for a plant ensemble,
you can also choose younger and smaller plants.

STYLING TIP

The rubber tree is a highlight in any kind of setting. However, make sure it does not stand out because of a thick layer of dust on its glossy leaves. The plant is even more decorative when its leaves shine and gleam. Simply dust the leaves with a damp cloth once a week. Extra tip: if you clean the leaves with a mixture of one part water and one part milk, they will have an extra bling effect due to the fat in the liquid.

∨ *Over-the-top jungle: gathering all your plants together not only creates a true urban jungle, but also makes it easier to water and care for them.*

∨ *Glossy: the leaves of the rubber tree shine at least as much as the brass lamp.*

IN FRONT OF A DARK WALL,
THE BEAUTIFUL CALATHEA
BECOMES A PIECE OF
LIVING ART.

STYLING TIP

Prayer plants are a great asset for any plantgang. If you have many green houseplants, add a purple or burgundy Calathea for a touch of colour and more variety. Colourful and patterned varieties of Calathea look particularly beautiful in front of colourful walls, like grey, dusty pink or indigo blue.

∨ *Calathea love high humidity. Arrangements with several houseplants create a micro climate with a slightly higher humidity, which is beneficial for both the plants and the room.*

∧ *Calathea thrive in indirect light, like in this kitchen corner.*

MORGANE & ARMAND

Toulouse / France

A GREEN NEST IN TOULOUSE

What do wool and plants have in common? They both bring warmth and life to a home.
In Toulouse, la ville rose (the pink city) in the South of France, Morgane just moved into a new apartment
with her son Armand. Together, wool and plants are the red – or should we say green? – thread running
through their lives and their home.

∨ *Family bliss for two: Morgane and Armand in their green Toulouse home.*

Morgane grew up surrounded by unfinished knitting projects and woollen blankets from her mom, as well as plants that were continually exchanged between family members. The women in her family were never far from either knitting needles or plants. Her aunt, a horticulturist, took Morgane to local markets to sell garden plants, and her mom taught her how to recognize plants by their flowers and leaves.

This became a natural way of life: wherever she goes, her eyes are always peeled for interesting plants and cuttings that she can bring home and grow from there. The plants make her and Armand's apartment come to life and are worthy companions.

PLANTS ARE THE BINDING ELEMENT IN MORGANE'S FAMILY. AND ARMAND HAS INHERITED HIS MOTHER'S LOVE FOR PLANTS, TOO.

< *Hung above each other, both Oxalis and Pilea use the limited space.*
∨ *Even in the small kitchen, plants are at home.*

∨ *Cosy get-together: the fiddle leaf fig sets the tone while the various succulents, the Pilea, the Oxalis and the little home-grown avocado tree listen carefully.*

MORGANE INHERITED
SOME OF THE PLANTS
FROM HER MOTHER.
THESE ARE PRECIOUS
HEIRLOOMS.

When looking for a new apartment, one of Morgane's criteria was to find a luminous place, preferably with a little outdoor space, that would be ideal for the large collection of plants that she had gathered over the years. And that's exactly what she found: a bright space with enough room for Armand to play, for her plants to thrive and for her to work on creative projects. To take full advantage of the light, there are no curtains in the apartment – and her plants thank her for that.

Morgane splits her time between working as a dietician at a hospital and working as a creative professional. She creates DIY projects for brands and companies, often using her favourite materials: wool and plants. Since she works from home, all her creative tools, such as weaving loom, knitting needles, bundles of wool and scissors are automatically part of the décor. She even knitted some plant pots for her green friends.

COOL IDEA

The botanical theme is perpetual in this home. Plants are accompanied by paper garlands with leaf patterns and beautiful botanical frames with leaves (see DIY instructions on page 118).

> *A relaxed atmosphere in the bedroom with botanical art.*

∧ *The paper garland is by French artist Virginie Sannier-Dorémieux (Mi-avril).*

< *Shelving made of crates offers plenty of space for both wool and plants.*

∨ *Wild West atmosphere in Armand's room: a play tent, his cuddly toys and of course plants embellish the room.*

The most beloved plants in Morgane's collection come from her late mother. They are the living heritage that keeps bringing joy to their lives while reminding them of their mother and grandmother. The big Rhipsalis cactus on the shelves in the living room didn't grow very well at her mom's place a few years ago. She and her brother each got a cutting, and both grew to be strong and healthy. The Rhipsalis now lives together with a collection of vintage cups, more wool and thread, little objects, vases with faces and some vintage figurines, which quite literally add a lot of character to the beautifully styled plantshelves.

Sprinkled around the house, you'll find upcycled Duralex glassware. At flea markets and in thrift shops in France, you can easily find vintage Duralex glasses and bowls that have a beautiful diamond shape. If you spray-paint them with matte paint, they look just like ceramics. The cups are ideal for small cacti, and the bigger bowls make nice saucers for bigger plant pots.

UPCYCLING FOR PLANTS: SPRAY-PAINT VINTAGE DURALEX GLASSWARE AND YOU'LL GET FUNKY NEW PLANT VESSELS.

> Armand loves to romp around – but he's
careful with mum's plants!

TENDING TO MY
PLANTS IS MY WEEKLY RITUAL.
IT IS MY PERSONAL
TIME OUT.

< *Morgane's Monstera deliciosa stretches out for some extra rays of sun.*
∨ *Combining her love for wool and plants with a hand-knitted plant pot cover.*

∨ *Morgane covered her vintage chest of drawers with a textile with a botanical print, creating a real highlight in the living room.*

COOL IDEA

*Why not upgrade a vintage piece of furniture with
a botanical theme? The fronts of furniture can easily be covered
with either textiles or leftover wallpaper with botanical patterns
for a real eye-catching effect!*

Morgane and Armand's home feels like a cosy nest: instead of a couch Morgane chose to install a daybed in the living room. It is covered with lots of warm blankets, cushions and Armand's bears. She decorated the apartment with her own creations, some of Armand's drawings and handmade pieces by dear friends, like the Chapoleone hats on the wall (by Camille Agar), the Mi-avril paper garland (by Virginie Sannier-Dorémieux) and postcards by Saar Manche (who is also the illustrator of this book) and Audrey Jeanne.

Morgane has a weakness for Sedum and Aeonium – she regularly buys the same species of a plant she already owns, simply because she cannot resist it. Amongst mature, full-grown plants are small vases with cuttings that are growing new roots in water. These new babies are waiting to be exchanged with her plant-loving friends and family. One of the plants that is particularly suited to exchanging with others is the Pilea peperomioides, also known as the pancake plant or Chinese money plant. It's a true blogger superstar, and giving a little offshoot to someone is a token of luck. The big Pilea in the plant hanger is the mother of her other Pilea plant on top of the wooden crates. It's one of Morgane's favourite plants, because its small babies continue to grow in other people's homes.

**I GROW LITTLE PLANT
BABIES IN GLASS JARS.
THESE SERVE AS PERSONAL
GREEN GIFTS FOR FAMILY AND
FRIENDS. EXCEPTIONALLY
WELL SUITED IS THE
PILEA PEPEROMIOIDES.**

↗ *Playful details between a Rhipsalis and reels of thread.*
˃ *The green Oxalis looks like an ever-growing lucky charm.*

< *Morgane adores the serenity during her weekly plant-care session.*
∨ *Wool and plants all over the place.*
> *Viva Mexico! Armand knows the plants and is aware of a cactus's spiky nature. But to be on the safe side, the Trichocerus is encaged.*

Watering the plants is a weekly ritual that Morgane wants to keep for herself. Armand sometimes helps her, but she is so attached to her plants that she prefers to care for them herself. It's a very soothing activity which calms her. Every now and then she adds a scoop of fresh organic soil or some natural fertilizer grains to keep her plants healthy and in good shape. (She doesn't use liquid fertilizer, as she wants to keep the air in the apartment as healthy as possible.)

The only plant missing in their home is a big elephant ear plant (Colocasia) – Morgane dreams of owning one! She and Armand regularly visit greenhouses and nurseries near their hometown of Toulouse, and she thinks the big elephant ear plants they see there would make a nice addition to their home. But until then, she'll take good care of their hundred plants.

Morgane's love for plants comes full circle with Armand: when they visit local nurseries and garden centres, he often reminds his mother that they "don't own that particular plant yet" and they "should bring it home". He is very careful with the plants, too: the home is a safe haven for all its occupants.

→ *Find out more about Morgane at www.morganours.com*

DID YOU KNOW

that the Oxalis is edible? The leaves and flowers can be eaten raw or cooked, and have a slightly sour taste. But beware: the Oxalis is toxic to cats!

∨ Weaving is Morgane's second passion. She creates decorative wall hangings for her own home and for clients.

5 QUESTIONS

FOR MORGANE

1 Where does your love for plants come from?
Plants have been such a natural part of my life. When I was growing up, there were always plants and cuttings everywhere, at home and in our relatives' homes. It's part of our family tradition to exchange plants and cuttings.

2 What do plants mean to you?
They give me companionship and bring liveliness to a home.

3 How would you describe your home/interior styling? Are you aiming for a certain style?
I don't know if there is a name for my interior style. It's a mix of bohemian, Scandinavian, romantic, contemporary, colourful and vintage. Although less vintage than it was a few years ago. I'm aiming for a more light and contemporary style in this new apartment. But it will never be minimal.

4 What do you look for when you're in the mood for a new plant at home? Where do you find them?
I always keep my eyes peeled for anything that grows! When looking for new plants, I want to be surprised by an interesting shape or colour. I never look for rarity, but for something fun and upbeat that makes me smile.

5 You have wonderful plant pots at home. Where do you source them?
Most of my plant pots come from thrift stores, charity shops and flea markets. I love all these old terracotta pots with mineral deposits that are imperfect and have character. For my birthday, I received this beautiful pot from Group Partner as a gift (see page 114) and I also really like to update thrifted Duralex glassware with spray paint. I use matte spray paint, which makes them look like ceramics (see page 104).

STYLING TIP

Children's furniture from the flea market as an alternative to a plant stand? Why not!

MAKE YOUR OWN BOTANICAL FRAME

Highlight the graphic beauty of a plant leaf
with this very easy-to-make botanical frame.

v *Inspired by the transparent frames of the Danish
brand Moebe, Morgane created this plant picture
with two sheets of glass, thick black tape and an
artificial leaf.*

YOU NEED:

- Two identical sheets of glass or Plexiglas.
- Black electrical tape, or thick washi tape. If the tape is too thin, the glass edges will cut right through it.
- A fake leaf (fabric or silk). You can also use a real leaf, but the result won't last as long and the leaf may be squished between the sheets of glass. A good natural alternative is a dried leaf.
- Scissors.

1 Remove the wire and plastic stems from the fake leaf. The leaf should be as thin as possible.

2 Position the leaf on one sheet of glass. Delicately place the second sheet of glass on top. Make sure you don't cut your fingers on the edges of the glass.

3 Tape the edges of the two sheets of glass together. Start with the two longest sides of the frame. Neatly cut off the tape at the angles. Finish with the two shorter sides of the frame.

4 All done! Admire the result and give your plant frame a nice spot on your shelf.

TRADESCANTIA

SPIDERWORT

The Tradescantia belongs to the family of Commelinaceae and is a genus that includes common climbing and trailing houseplants like the Wandering Jew, purple heart and Moses in the cradle. The three-petalled spiderwort flowers are usually blue to purple, but may also be pink, white or red.

ᵥ *Pretty and playful – the colours of the Tradescantia perfectly
match earthy hues and vintage ceramics.*

A flower of the Tradescantia only blooms for one day, open-ing its petals in the morning and closing them at night. Plants with multiple flowers will bloom continually for up to four to six weeks in summer. Tradescantia houseplants partially owe their popularity to their distinctive colours and patterns, which bring an additional touch to the green plants spectrum: from deep burgundy hues to shades of purple and zebra stripes (Tradescantia zebrina). The purple heart plant, a more common name of the Tradescantia pallida, for example, stands out because of its special colours, with reflecting shimmers and all kinds of colours between purple and green. Tradescantia is a perennial, herbaceous plant native to eastern Mexico, but is also a popular houseplant and ornamental plant in frost-free gardens.

DID YOU KNOW

*that Tradescantia's beautiful colouring
depends on its location and care? If the plant
does not get enough sunlight or receives
too much fertilizer, its leaves will turn green
and lose their unique look. So make sure
that the plant gets enough light,
and use fertilizer sparingly!*

Spiderwort are very undemanding houseplants. Besides an abundance of light, preferably direct sunlight, they don't require a lot of care. You can stick to the motto "less is more". Less water, less fertilizer, and your Tradescantia will be happy. The plant is also particularly easy to multiply: you can grow new plants from small cuttings without too much effort. Within a short period of time, a young plant or cuttings can grow considerably. Initially, the plant grows upright, but under the weight of the leaves, it will then drop its stems down to all sides. Therefore, Tradescantia are exceptionally suited for hanging baskets or on wall shelves. Some people say that these plants are like weeds and that this makes them less attractive. But we as plant lovers truly enjoy the wild jungle look of a big, healthy Tradescantia!

⌐ *Styling: ochre, blue and the dark purple of a Tradescantia make for great visual harmony in front of a grey wall.*

∧ *Detail: the leaves feature hues from dark green to deep purple.*

> *The flowers of the Tradescantia are small, fragile and mostly soft pink or purple.*

CARE TIPS:

☀ *Location: Very bright, even direct sunlight. Perfect for south-facing windows and potting in hanging baskets.*

🌡 *Temperature: Normal room temperature. The plant does not tolerate frost.*

💧 *Watering: Water sparingly when the top layer of soil has dried out. In winter, water less frequently.*

♡ *Fertilizer: Liquid fertilizer once a month in the summer, ideally half the recommended dose.*

PILEA
PEPEROMIOIDES

PLANT PORTRAIT

CHINESE MONEY PLANT

Now this is a very special plant: the Pilea peperomioides, often simply referred to as Pilea.
This plant is a real blogging superstar, having been featured on many blogs from all over the world.
It started on Scandinavian design blogs and soon made it all across the world
in various interior stylings.

< *The Pilea enriches this nature-inspired still life.*
∨ *The round leaves sit on long stems that grow in all directions. Thus, a Pilea makes the perfect eye-catcher on any sideboard.*

T he funny-looking plant with its round leaves that resemble floating UFOs or pancakes (it is also called the pancake plant) quickly got a lot of hype on social media and left people wondering: What is this plant? What is it called? And how can I get one? The latter proved to be a bit tricky, as the Pilea is rarely sold in conventional garden centres.

Pilea peperomioides belongs to the family of Urticaceae plants of the genus Pilea. Its native habitat is the Yunan province in southern China. There the Pilea grows and thrives in shady, humid spots in forests at a higher altitude, and is a rather rare species. As a houseplant, it is widely popular all around the world, despite the fact

DID YOU KNOW

that the Pilea is also called "Missionary Plant"? A Norwegian missionary brought the first specimen from China to Norway in 1944 when he had to leave China. In Norway, the missionary gave offshoots to fascinated friends and family members.

that its presence in shops and garden centres is sometimes as rare as its natural occurrence. The Chinese money plant is a rather unpretentious houseplant, but prefers a constant ambient temperature (normal room temperature). It is advised to keep the plant at around 10°C during winter in order to foster its blooming, which yet again is a rather seldom appearance indoors. The Pilea likes to be watered regularly, but dislikes soggy soil. Another great predisposition of the plant is its easy propagation. It constantly grows new shoots that can easily be separated from the mother plant and offered to family and friends as a green gift. This might be one reason why the plant is rarely sold – it simply multiplies itself too easily!

∧ *Botanical trio: a Dracaena, a Pilea and a botanical art print unite for a coherent overall picture.*

> *The Pilea often produces offshoots that grow into sturdy young plants.*

CARE TIPS:

Location: Bright to semi-shaded. In partial shade the leaves will grow bigger. Under ideal conditions these can grow up to the size of your palm.

Temperature: Normal room temperature. To stimulate blooming, this should ideally be kept at around 10°C during winter.

Watering: Water regularly, while avoiding soggy soil. Also avoid letting the soil dry out. Too much water will lead to rotting roots, while conditions that are too dry will make the leaves turn yellow and eventually fall off.

Fertilizer: During summer, use liquid fertilizer.

TRADESCANTIA & PILEA

STYLING TIPS

The Pilea is a beautiful accent plant on any shelf, sideboard or windowsill. Due to her long stems and round leaves, she has a very ornamental look and sets visual highlights in interiors. The Tradescantia, on the other hand, convinces with her rich colours and patterns. On a side note: Both plants are ideal for hanging planters, too!

DID YOU KNOW

that the Pilea peperomioides was practically unknown to botanists until the 1980s? The first known published picture of the plant appeared in the English magazine "Kew" in 1984.

∧ *The dainty Pilea cuts a fine figure on a kitchen shelf, too. Plant it in a cup and add a green spot to your kitchen shelf.*

⊐ *Happy trio: the dachshund enjoys the green company. Lovely idea: put the potted Pilea in a paper bag for an unusual look.*

THE PILEA IS PERFECTLY SUITED FOR A BOTANICAL FAMILY PORTRAIT. SIMPLY REMOVE THE OFFSHOOTS FROM THE MOTHER PLANT AND PUT THEM IN SEPARATE LITTLE POTS. THEN ARRANGE THEM TOGETHER WITH THE MOTHER PLANT FOR A FUN GREEN FAMILY PORTRAIT.

∧ A dramatic plant styling using a
 collection of vintage ceramics on
 a string shelf and hanging plants
 in macramé hangers.

∨ Why not style up your bar cart with plants instead of bottles and glasses? With its trailing stems and colourful leaves, the Tradescantia is an ideal choice.

Porzellan Manufaktur Nymphenburg

The Shopkeeper's Home   Caroline Rowland

MÜNCHEN   Christine Bauer
Interiors und Stadträume   Wolfgang Kehl

< *A second life for old cans as hanging retro planters, here in the home of Dutch illustrator Ruth Hengeveld.*
∨ *From small to big: baby plants in terracotta pots, a terrarium and a wild Tradescantia flock playfully on a sideboard.*

∨ *Tone-on-tone: the young Tradescantia mingles with a purple Echeveria and a matching amethyst.*

IF YOU HAVE CHOSEN A TRADESCANTIA FOR ITS VIBRANT COLOURS, MAKE SURE IT GETS ENOUGH SUNLIGHT. IT IS ONLY THEN THAT THE PLANT ACHIEVES ITS FULL EFFECT AND COLOURING.

FEM, SAN & SEZER

Istanbul / Turkey

A PLANT PARADISE ABOVE ISTANBUL'S ROOFTOPS

In Istanbul's leafy and hilly Besiktas district, on the European side of the Turkish megalopolis, the view opens up over the Bosporus towards Asia. But it's not the fantastic view that has brought us to buzzing Istanbul: this is the home of Fem Güclütürk and her "little" green patchwork family comprised of son San, partner Sezer and about 600 houseplants!

∧ *Plant and family bliss in Istanbul:*
the patchwork family consists of Sezer,
plant expert Fem and her son San.

F em is a woman with an infectious smile – her zest for life is almost tangible when you meet her in person. What also seems almost tangible is her passionate love for plants. This love not only defines her professional life as the founder and manager of the plant studio Labofem – it definitely defines her entire life.

After a stellar career in public relations and some changes in her personal life, Fem decided to take the leap and turn her life inside out. She left the PR business with nothing but an industrial stool she liked from the office (it now serves as a plant stand, of course) and let her passion guide the way: she opened a plant studio called Labofem, which was initially in her apartment as a sort of "open studio". However, the open-house situation soon took over her entire private life – plants were everywhere, and clients were constantly making requests for visits. It was then that she separated her private and business life by opening a nearby plant studio. Even though home and the workplace are separated now, her life is still strongly dominated by plants in both places.

MY HOME WAS A PLANT STUDIO AND OPEN HOUSE FOR A LONG TIME. TODAY I RUN A PLANT STUDIO NAMED LABOFEM NOT FAR FROM MY HOME.

∨ Fem's shop Labofem bursts with green: from hanging kokedama to leafy species and intriguing terrariums. Every plant lover is sure to find a treasure here.

∧ Come in: the plant studio Labofem swings open its doors and welcomes plant enthusiasts from Istanbul and around the world.

COOL IDEA

Display your plants differently: Why not plant your little cacti and succulents in unusual planters? How about some vintage ceramic mugs sourced at the flea market, or old coffee cups, big shells or DIY painted terracotta pots? Whether you prefer to stick to one style or go for the mix & match look – plant fun and curious looks will be guaranteed!

The modern studio has become an integral part of Fem's daily life. This is the place where she gets creative and comes up with new plant-pot combinations, sells plants in situ and online; and meets customers, plant lovers, business partners and ceramicists. And what you see in her eyes is not about business – it is a devotion to plants and a deep respect for them as living beings. She often refers to them as her kids and honestly admits that parting with plants that are sold can be tough at times. Even though there is lots to sell and give away: her studio boasts all kind of plants, from small cacti and succulents to vibrant ferns, peculiar air plants and leafy philodendrons, all paired with unusual and often one-of-a-kind pots made by local ceramicists or sourced globally. Fem has a very precise idea of how the plant-pot combinations should look and gives detailed instructions to collaborating ceramicists. Sometimes, she also gets things done herself by painting and recreating conventional plant pots. Even though her plant sales are limited to the metropolitan area of Istanbul, she welcomes plant enthusiasts from around the world who have heard of Labofem. And local customers who order online often get a chance to say hello to Fem in person as she delivers plants on her Vespa, manoeuvring through the dense Istanbul traffic.

MY PLANTS TRAVEL BACK AND FORTH FROM THE STUDIO TO MY APARTMENT – ALWAYS ACCORDING TO THEIR NEEDS!

↗ *Small cacti in handmade ceramic vessels made by selected Turkish ceramicists.*
> *Graphic patterns and vivid colours side by side with neutral hues.*

< *The wooden vintage table holds a vibrant collection of cacti, succulents and handmade terracotta pots from Fem's last trip to Sri Lanka.*
∨ *The upper floor features a gardening corner for daily plant care at home.*

Plants are the connecting element between Fem's studio and her home. The apartment covers two floors, with large balconies overlooking the Bosporus. For Fem Güclütürk, her home is an eclectic gem and a visual "business card" – hundreds of plants dwell in the various rooms, side by side with memorabilia from her many trips to Africa, Asia and South America. The absence of plants is a non-existing concept in Fem's understanding of a happy life. According to her, the key to success in living with plants is having profound respect for your plants and listening to them. "Even though plants are quiet living beings, you can learn to listen to them," she explains. Her plants are far more than a decorative element – she observes them and detects any kind of change they expose. "Everyone should try to understand the plants' language," concludes Fem.

With hundreds of different plants, plant care takes a few hours. Luckily she is an early bird and gets up between 5 and 6 a.m., before the rest of the family. The early hours are used to tend

DID YOU KNOW

that some plants can get sunburned? Don't leave your plants unprotected and exposed to the full sun during the summer. A light curtain or blinds will do the trick.

I DON'T LOOK AT MY PLANTS
AS DECORATIVE OBJECTS.
RATHER, I LOOK AT THEM WITH
LOVE AND CARE – JUST LIKE
A PERSON I LOVE.

EVERYBODY SHOULD
TRY TO LEARN THE LANGUAGE
OF PLANTS. I DO NOT
SPEAK TO MY PLANTS –
I LISTEN TO THEM.

∧ *Jungle fever in the bedroom: A vintage mannequin,
old leather suitcases and a bushy Dracaena reflexa
accompanied by some large potted cacti.*

∨ The bedroom balcony is reserved for cacti and succulents. Particularly the Echeveria seems to particularly enjoy its airy location.

∧ *The lounge area is ideal for semi-shade-loving plants.*
 Thriving in freedom: this Syngonium has all the space it needs to spread out its green arms.

to her plants: she checks up on all the plants, waters and sprays them if necessary, cleans them and removes wilted leaves. The plant-care routine lasts until roughly 10 a.m., with a break for a vivacious family breakfast that acts as an additional energy boost for Fem. Later, she takes off to the nearby studio and continues her green mission at Labofem.

It's not uncommon to see Fem juggling plants back and forth between her home and studio. Sometimes, she takes plants back home for some extra care and light therapy, as the home has a better light situation due to its top-floor position. On the upper floor, she even has an extra studio where she repots plants and treats them if they show signs of feebleness. Even friends bring their flagging plants to her home for some extra care. The large balcony provides an additional space with fresh air and sunlight, and this is also the place where Fem grows some veggies, herbs and strawberries. The lower floor is reserved for enjoying family life, surrounded by yet more plants and lots of unusual travel souvenirs from around the globe.

STYLING TIP

Plant stylings are no different to any other styling projects. It is the combination of colours, shapes, sizes and textures that makes the difference. Keep in mind that not only the pots, but the plants themselves, have a visual impact. Think glossy leaves combined with spiky cacti or marbled leaf patterns. At the beginning, put everything together and then take away whatever doesn't fit, one by one. The result should be a well-composed vignette with one visual highlight, e.g. a dominant plant, an unusual planter or a salient décor object.

I HAVE GROWN MY
PLANTS OVER THE YEARS.
TODAY, I CANNOT IMAGINE
OUR HOME WITHOUT
PLANTS.

∧ *Cactus Symphony No. 9:
art, plants and music unite in
a beautiful composition.*

I LOVE AND RESPECT PLANTS.
A HOME WITHOUT PLANTS
IS LIKE A DISMAL, EMPTY
DESERT TO ME.

COOL IDEA

Plant care is more fun with nice gear. Invest in beautiful accessories to make your plant-care sessions even more pleasant: a lovely watering can, special gardening shears, little spades, watering bulbs and more. Plant care will not only be more fun, but more stylish too!

⌐ *The rooftop terrace is a real urban jungle and overlooks the nearby Bosporus.*
∧ *Fem tends to her plants with love and respect.*
< *The terrace boasts plants and features shamrocks as well as strawberries.*

Visiting Fem in Istanbul in either her home or studio leaves a lasting impression. Her passion for plants and her respect towards them, as well as the vibrant, loving and fun family life in her home, seem to spread like fire. It leaves the visitor wondering: does this unlimited source of energy stem from the many happy plants or from Fem's vivid personality? Whatever the correct answer is, one thing is clear: both energies meet in this warm and beautiful green home. It seems almost poetic and natural in a city like Istanbul, where Europe and Asia meet.

5 QUESTIONS
FOR FEM

EXPERT TIPS

1 Where does your love for plants come from?

In Turkey we have an ancient relationship with plants and nature. The tree of life is still part of our Anatolian culture. Our great-grandmothers and grandfathers were shamans. We still have some superstitions: symbols and habits which we think are part of Muslim religion, but are not. These were merged into our daily life and became a habit over the years – things like binding coloured ropes to trees, knocking on wood, having "kilims" with wild animals, etc. Our ancestors used to live in harmony with nature, and to respect it. Our land is very fertile, so it was natural to live in and with nature harmoniously. But with migration to big cities, technology and the difficulties of urban living made our generation lose its connection to nature. We check the weather not by looking into the sky, but with AccuWeather! How silly! Now, we all need to rebuild that "love and respect" connection to all living creatures, and touch the soil again. My love for plants is a very natural way of life for me and for my family.

2 What does living with plants mean to you?

They fascinate me more than human beings. Plants can survive without us, as they did for millions years, but people and animals can't survive a day without them. They are astonishing in their ability to adapt, their reproduction, their beauty and of course their shape and form. They are silent, and yet you can still listen to them. I love, adore and respect them. A house without plants is like a desert to me: empty, dead, soulless.

3 You live and work with plants in both your home and your studio. Is there a real difference between your home and your studio?

They complement each other, actually. My house windows are exposed to both east and west, so plants from the shaded studio come back home for therapy! Up until 2014, I sold the plants in my "open house" apartment. But after awhile, plants were taking over the house. We were like guests in our own home and couldn't move properly. So I decided that I had to open a studio, not far from home. Now, my home feels like an intimate home again, and the studio is really a place to work.

4 Which plants do you have at home?

Did you see my home story? I have approximately 600 pots with different plants at home. It's impossible to name them all. Amongst the bigger ones are several Monstera, Areca palms, Dracaena, Sansevieria, Caryota mitis, Euphorbia...

5 Do you have a favourite plant? If so, why?

I always ask myself that same question. It's like if you ask me which food I like the most or which destination I most like to travel to – all these questions are difficult to answer. I love ferns for their attitude. I also love tropical plants, palms and philodendrons (for their leaves). I respect succulents for their power to survive, and I love weeds for their healing power. The list is endless!

KOKEDAMA

Blogger and stylist Tiffany Grant-Riley from the blog
Curate & Display shows us how easy it is to make your
own kokedama, or Japanese moss balls.

∧ *Japanese moss balls, also known as
kokedama, are perfectly suited for
humidity-loving plants like ferns or ivy.*

YOU'LL NEED:

- *Moisture-loving plants, like ferns, ivy or orchids*
- *Sphagnum moss*
- *All-purpose compost*
- *Bonsai or Akadama soil*
- *Garden twine, string or thin cord*
- *Sheet moss*

1 *Gently remove the excess soil from the root ball of the plant. Wrap the root ball in moist sphagnum moss.*

2 *Combine equal parts of the compost and soil in a bucket, adding a little water so it holds together. Shape the mixture into a ball big enough to house the roots of your plant. You'll need to squeeze some of the moisture out of the soil as you do this.*

3 *Make a hole in the centre of the soil ball and carefully insert the moss-wrapped roots of the plant into it. Press it more firmly together if it falls apart, and set it in the centre of the sheet of moss.*

4 *Bring the sides of the sheet moss up around the ball of soil, removing any excess folds, and secure it by wrapping the string firmly around it. When you've sufficiently wrapped the ball, knot the string. Tie three additional lengths of string onto the kokedama, and it's ready to hang up! Water your kokedama roughly once a week – by submerging it in water or spritzing it with a plant mister – so that the moss doesn't dry out.*

Find out more about Tiffany at curateanddisplay.co.uk

PALMS

For most of us living in the temperate zones of the world, palm trees (Arecaceae or Palmae) are the epitome of the exotic: in our mind's eye we connect palms with tropical beaches, dream voyages and far-away paradises. The natural habitat of palms lies between the 40th parallel north and the 44th parallel south, encompassing a large zone from southern France to the Chatham Islands that belong to New Zealand.

STYLING TIP

Palm trees are excellent statement pieces in a home because of their size. They like big, tall plant pots because their roots like to dig deep into the ground. To mask the exposed soil in the large pot, you can wrap a nice piece of fabric (perhaps one that matches your throw cushions or interior's colour palette) around the rim of the pot. Also note the particularly beautiful shadows palms create on the wall and floor when the sun comes out!

∧ *Oriental flair created with a palm, a patterned wall hanging and a golden décor object for extra bling.*

> *If you don't have a large plant pot, simply put your palm tree in a decorative basket.*

In places where palms don't grow naturally, they are cultivated in tall 19th-century glasshouses or in offices, shopping malls and homes, almost always as undersized versions of their true selves.

In the tropics and subtropics, palm trees are part of the natural vegetation and therefore part of everyday life. Some kinds of palms have been of huge importance to the local economies of certain countries and the survival of their people, because they provide precious calories, fibres and building material. The settlement of the archipelagos in the Pacific Ocean would not have been possible without the coconut water contained in coconuts. It enabled people to survive on islands in the South Sea that were completely surrounded by salt water. Three to six unripe coconuts were sufficient to meet one person's water requirements for a day at tropical temperatures.

If you're looking for a palm tree that is adapted to your climate, a local garden centre is the place to go. Or you can try and grow your own palm tree with seeds from your holiday destination in the Mediterranean or from a tropical island. You should be aware that growing a palm tree requires a lot of patience, but at the same time it's fascinating to observe the growth of your own baby palm tree.

The tiny roots and leaves of a small plant are already very strong and may help you understand how palm trees can grow up to 30 metres high with rather slim trunks.

∨ *Reaching high: the Kentia palm tree in this bedroom stretches towards the ceiling. Younger palm trees can be displayed on sideboards and create an instant tropical vibe in any room.*

CARE TIPS:

Location: In direct sunlight (but not all day!) or a bright location. The perfect spot is near a window or in any south-facing room. In their natural habitat smaller plants, are protected from direct sunlight by larger vegetation, which means two to three hours of direct sunlight per day is enough for potted palm trees.

Temperature: Room temperature. Avoid drafts. Some outdoor palms tolerate lows of -22°C. But try to keep indoor palms at a minimum of 13°C.

Watering: Most palms require fair amounts of water. Water generously, make sure the excess water runs freely through the drainage holes. The cooler the room, the less water the tree needs.

Fertilizer: Follow instructions for specific palms. Usually every 15 days during the growth period. No fertilizer in the winter.

SANSEVIERIA

SNAKE PLANT

The Sansevieria, also known as snake plant, is truly one of the easiest houseplants.
The succulent plant stores water in its sturdy long leaves and is absolutely low-maintenance: the plant is
forgiving if you forget to water it from time to time, and thrives even in darker corners of your home.
But more light will result in a brighter colour and richer patterns
on its leaves, as well as faster growth.

Sansevieria originate in tropical Africa, although there are some species growing in Asia as well. The Sansevieria is commonly called the snake plant because of the shape of its leaves – or even mother-in-law's tongue because of the leaves' sharpness. The name Sansevieria, however, comes from the Prince of Sanseviero, Raimondo de Sango (1710–1771), a particularly tough and strong scientist and plant lover from Naples.

Sansevieria are tough: their roots are strong and can easily break a plant pot that is too small. Try to avoid this by repotting if the plant becomes root-bound, which you will see if the plant rises in the pot or roots appear on the surface.

We distinguish between two kinds of Sansevieria: the tall, lance-shaped plants, which are most common, and the smaller dwarf plants, which grow in rosettes. Most Sansevieria have beautifully speckled leaves in deep shades of green, and some species, like the Sansevieria trifasciata "Laurentii", have distinctive yellow or silvery-white stripes on the edges of the leaves.

DID YOU KNOW

that the snake plant is ideal for the bedroom?
It absorbs carbon dioxide and converts
it into fresh oxygen, which is released at night.
Thus, the snake plant supports better
and healthier sleep.

∧ *The Sansevieria has an elegant look, thanks to its long, straight leaves. It creates a linear clarity in any styling.*

< *Thanks to its versatility when it comes to light, a snake plant can either be placed on a sunny windowsill or in a semi-shaded corner of your home.*

Try to not touch the spiky top of the leaves: if this breaks off, the leaf will stop growing. Also, although snake plants can cope with almost any lightning situation, they don't like to be moved from darker to brighter places at once. If you want to move your plant to a place with a different light intensity, do this gradually so that the plant can adjust to it and avoid leaf burn from sunlight.

Sanseviera is a popular houseplant in houses, apartments, businesses and offices. In parts of Africa though, the plant has a greater, mystical meaning: it is used as a protective charm against evil or bewitchment and the leaves are used for fibre production. The leaves also have antiseptic qualities that are used for bandages in traditional first aid.

∨ *The lush green hues of the plants accentuate the airy and inviting look of this room in Arizona. The plants have been aptly placed in three corners and set equal visual accents across the room.*

CARE TIPS:

Location: Practically anywhere, from bright spots to shaded ones.

Temperature: Warm, between 18°C and 27°C. The temperature should never go below 13°C.

Watering: Water sparsely. Sansevieria will rot when overwatered. They are particularly draught-tolerant, wait if in doubt.

Fertilizer: Once every month during the growth period, diluted by 50%. The plants don't need to be repotted very often – they like to fit tightly into their pot. Instead of repotting, you can remove a few centimetres of soil and replace it with fresh soil that covers the exposed roots.

SANSEVIERIA & PALMS

STYLING TIPS

Both Sansevieria and palms tend to be rather big, upward-growing plants. While palms create an instant tropical feeling, the snake plant revives a retro vibe and pairs well with other houseplants. Palms, on the other hand, are perfect solo players which need space and freedom to fully unleash their tropical palm fronds. Both plants usually require larger pots, which should be carefully considered for styling projects – pick the planters according to your interior style, as they will definitely stand out due to their size.

Palms are very decorative houseplants: they automatically bring a tropical vibe into a home. Today, over 2,500 species of palms belonging to 183 genera are known to botanical science. The most common ones for interior usage are the Livistona, Phoenix and Trachycarpus. Characteristic for all palm trees are their leaves, of which there are several different types: fan-shaped leaves, feather-shaped leaves and even undivided leaves. The various leaves give palms a very different look, which should be taken into consideration when buying a new plant for your home.

DID YOU KNOW

that palms are not trees in the botanical sense? Their trunks are made not of wood but of fibres, and thus they are more related to maize than to oaks.

∨ *A young Cycad sets a highlight in this living room. Even though it looks like a palm, botanically it doesn't belong to the Palmae.*

TROPICAL HOME: PALMS PLACED
IN FRONT OF A COLOURED
FEATURE WALL IN A WARM
HUE LOOK LIKE A VISUAL MINI
VACATION IN THE SOUTH.

∧ *Tropical feeling everywhere: the palm in
front of the orange wall recalls memories
of a tropical paradise.*

SMALLER SANSEVIERIA PLANTS
CAN BE DISPLAYED IN HANGING
PLANTERS AND ARE A GREAT
OPTION FOR SMALLER ROOMS
WITH DIFFICULT LIGHTING
SITUATIONS.

ᐯ *The Sansevieria trifasciata "Laurentii"
wins over with its yellow-green leaf
edges and enriches every plant
arrangement.*

< This Andy Warhol poster surveils a plantgang
with two small Sansevieria representatives.
∨ This large pencil cactus is only topped by the
big bushy snake plant.

STYLING TIP

The Sansevieria is particularly sculptural
and features a high, straight growth. Placed
alone or in a group of plants, it will add
a vertical accent in stylings.

"WHAT IS THE BEST PLANT FOR MY TINY APARTMENT? THERE ARE SO MANY PLANTS TO CHOOSE FROM, I DON'T KNOW WHERE TO START!"

HOW TO CREATE YOUR OWN URBAN JUNGLE

WHERE DO I START?

Believe us, we all kill a plant every now and then. Some plants are unhealthy when we buy them, or maybe they had a temperature shock between the grower, the store where we bought them and our home. And sometimes, we simply forget to water them. But the most common cause of plant-death: overwatering.

It's very understandable: when we buy a new plant we're excited and want to take good care of our new plant friend. We lavish it with care and attention, and give it a drink of water every day. But most plants only need to be watered once or twice a week - and some much less often. Our overeagerness turns out to be a fatal mistake, and the new plant bites the dust. As a side note, a tip: the finger test is always good. If the upper layer of soil is dry, you can water the plant again.

WHICH PLANT SHOULD I CHOOSE?

To make having your own urban jungle as much fun as possible, it's important that you choose a plant that you like (or better: love). There are so many species to choose from that it's easy to find a plant with a colour, pattern, shape or size that appeals to you aesthetically. It's also important that you choose a plant that fits your lifestyle. If you travel a lot and don't spend much time at home, you shouldn't pick plants that require lots of daily attention in the form of pruning, watering or fertilizing. Cacti and succulents might

be good choices for you. It's also important to choose a plant that will fit well into your home and find a good place in which to grow. What kind of light do you have at home? How much room is there? How warm or cool is it? All of these things should be considered when choosing a plant.

We truly believe that there is no such thing as a black thumb. If you are willing to invest a little bit of TLC (time, love and care) into your new green friend(s), and if you do your homework, you can have a healthy and thriving jungle at home. Let's start with the homework: when you purchase a new plant, keep the tag. Or, if you don't like the tag (we agree: most of the time they are rather ugly), simply snap a picture of your plant and its tag with your phone for future reference. Then simply google the name of your plant to find some basic care tips on the internet. Also find the right spot for your plant (on your windowsill, in indirect sunlight, in a darker spot, draught-free, in a humid bathroom…) and water according to the instructions.

USEFUL WATERING TOOLS:

"BUT I ALWAYS FORGET TO WATER MY PLANTS!"

Our advice is simple: set an alarm on your phone or mark a certain day of the week in your calendar. Choose a "plant-care day" when you have a little more time available. Be aware, however, that the changing seasons often require a change in the rhythm of plant care. Fluctuations in the amount of sunlight, the temperature, or even draughts caused by an open window can influence how much water your plant needs. You will find that once your plants become part of your routine and lifestyle, you want to check in on them more often. How do they look? Are the leaves hanging down, or has their colour changed? Is the soil dry? It is so rewarding to see your plants thrive when you take good care of them. Maybe they will even reward you with some blooming!

Waterworks
A natural hydration system consisting of a partially glazed terracotta cone and a glass bulb with a cork stopper.

Parrot Flower Power
A connective device that keeps track of water, sunlight and fertilizer and uses Bluetooth to send you information on your mobile phone.

Elho Aqua Care
A plastic reservoir ball that keeps your plant hydrated when you're on holiday.

Aquasticks
A water-absorbing stick suited for houseplants in decorative pots with a water reservoir (like typical orchid pots, for example).

EASY
DIY
IDEA

Place a tall glass filled with water next to your plant and use a nylon shoelace as a connection – stick one end of the shoelace in the water glass, and the other end into the soil of the plant. Your plant will be slowly and regularly watered while you are away.

EASY-CARE PLANTS FOR BEGINNERS

If you want to limit the risks: start easy!
These are some of the easiest plants.

1. **PEACE LILY** (*Spathiphyllum, on the left*)

2. **DEVIL'S IVY / POTHOS** (*Epipremnum aureum*)

3. **SNAKE PLANT** (*Sansevieria*)

4. **SPIDER PLANT** (*Chlorophytum comosum*)

5. **ALOE VERA** (*on the left*)

CONTRIBUTING "URBAN JUNGLE BLOGGERS"

A special thanks to these 18 international bloggers who contributed photos to the book. Be sure to check out their blogs and Instagram feeds too – they are so talented!

Vielen Dank! Merci mille fois ! Dankjulliewel! Thank you so much! ¡Muchas gracias! Dziękuję bardzo! Hvala puno! Grazie mille! Mange tak!

Anette Laurim / *Germany*
LOOK! PIMP YOUR ROOM
Favourite plant: Senecio rowleyanus
"Instead of regular flower pots I often use tall vases for plants."
lookpimpyourroom.com
@lookpimpyouroom
photos on pages: 29/30/41/42/161/165/169(3+5)

Anne Ji-Mi Herngaard / *Denmark*
LITTLE GREEN FINGERS
Favourite plant: Monstera deliciosa
"The more the merrier!"
littlegreenfingers.com
@littlegreenfingers
photos on pages: 32/33/60/121/124/125/131/164

Antonia Schmitz / *Germany*
CRAFTIFAIR
Favourite plant: Monstera Deliciosa
"I use my coffee grounds as a natural fertilizer for all of my plants – it works great."
craftifair.com
@craftifair
photos on pages: 44/62/86/87/98/101/153

Elena Gardin / *Spain & Italy*
FACING NORTH WITH GRACIA
Favourite plant: Tillandsia usneoides
"Style together plants from similar eco-systems – this helps to create both proper caring conditions and a stronger look."
facingnorthwithgracia.blogspot.com
@vidabarceloni
photos on pages: 45/62

Elske Leenstra / *The Netherlands*
ELSKE
Favourite plant: Tolmiea menziesii
"Use old tins as flowerpots, like I did with mine (see page 169). Easy and fast!"
elskeleenstra.nl
@elskeleenstra
photo on pages: 169(1)

Heather Young / *Great Britain*
GROWING SPACES
Favourite plant: Pilea peperomioides
"Customize your pots to give them a unique look – I paint plain terracotta paints with emulsion to make them better suited to the style of my home."
growingspaces.net
@heatheryounguk
photos on pages: 27/34/43/127/157

Ilaria Fatone / *France & Italy*
UN DUE TRE ILARIA
Favourite plant: Monstera deliciosa und Sukkulenten
"Try grouping your plants by size or type in the same place to create a jungle look with even a limited number of plants (this is also a practical tip: you won't forget to water any of them)."
unduetre-ilaria.com
@un23ilaria
photo on page: 38

Janneke Luursema / *The Netherlands*
A WAY OF SEEING
Favourite plant: I love them all, but the more character the better!
"I like to group my plants in vintage ceramics."
luursema.nl
@still_____ (7x underscore)
photos on pages: : 2/25/61/98

Jocelyn Hefner / *USA & Germany*
THE INNER INTERIOR
Favourite plant: Chlorophytum comosum
"Once you find a place where your plants thrive, keep them there. Try your best not to move them around – they are comfort creatures and love harmonious, balanced surroundings."
theinnerinterior.com
@jocelynhefner
photos on pages: 31/63/65/90/99/158/169(4)

Kasia Nowakowska / *Poland*

PAPIEROWY WYMIAR

Favourite houseplant: cacti & Hoyas

"Most of my houseplants grow through hydroponics. Using water instead of soil offers both you and your plants a lot of advantages – it is much healthier and simpler."

papierowywymiar.blogspot.com

photos on pages: 24/39/40

Line Stützer / *Denmark*

Favourite plant: Calathea orbifolia

"Think big! Don't be afraid to use big plants on your table or dresser. Even our big green friends can handle the spotlight."

@linestutzer

photos on pages: 69/93/94/100/126/ 130/163

Lisa Reck / *Germany*

IT'S PRETTY NICE

Favourite plant: Monstera deliciosa

"Reach various heights by working with plant stands and hanging displays to make the most out of every space."

itsprettynice.com

@itsprettynice

photo on page: 169(2)

Maren Teichert / *Germany*

MINZA WILL SOMMER

Favourite plant: Monstera deliciosa

"I prefer my plants grouped in plant pots of similar colours and materials for a plantgang look. I then combine them with props such as art, design items and books."

minzawillsommer.blogspot.de

@minzawillsommer

photos on pages: 71/130

Marlous Snijder / *The Netherlands*

OH MARIE!

Favourite plant: Anigozanthos

"Most plants hate cold or draughts. And dust! Once in a while I literally shower my plants, to wash off the dust that has gathered on their leaves."

ohmarie.nl

@ohmariemag

photo on page: 133

Mel Chesneau / *New Zealand & Sweden*

STYLED CANVAS

Favourite plant: Calathea orbifolia

"Sometimes the unlikeliest place is the perfect spot for our green friends, like on top of the fridge!"

styledcanvas.com

@styledcanvas

photos on pages: 30/43/44/92/94

Mina Stanojković / *Serbia*

Favourite plant: Epipremnum aureum

"Listen to your plants, because they are the wisest and complain the least. Once you give them what they want – a pot of their own, gentle humming of your favourite song or careful watering – they will reward you by springing up anew. Simple acts of nourishing always do the trick."

@nevolimruze

photos on pages: 28/29/165

Souraya Hassan / *The Netherlands*

BINTI HOME

Favourite houseplant: Areca Palme

"Mix and match different plants in terracotta pots for a Mediterranean look."

bintihomeblog.com

@bintihome

photos on pages: 37/70/90/153/162

Tiffany Grant-Riley / *Great Britain*

CURATE & DISPLAY

Favourite plant: Ficus elastica

Choose sculptural statement plants that will grow tall and draw the eye up – the bigger the better!

curateanddisplay.co.uk

@curatedisplay

photos on pages: 71/88/89/150/151

Igor Josifovic / *Germany*

HAPPY INTERIOR BLOG

Favourite plant: Crassula ovata & Howea forsteriana (Kentia palm)

"Plan your plant care on weekends with some good music. Water, light, nutrients and good vibes do wonders for your plants!"

happyinteriorblog.com

@igorjosif

photos on pages: 40/64/65/67/95/101/122/132/156/159 and 39/125/133/154 by Lina Skukauskė

Judith de Graaff / *France*

JOELIX.COM

Favourite plant: All cacti and palms

"Instead of fridge magnets or other trinkets, bring home a little plant cutting or some seeds from your holiday. These make the best souvenirs and will remind you of your travels all year round."

joelix.com

@joelixjoelix

photos on pages: 22/23/26/33/35/66/ 120/122/123/133/152/155/173

SHOPS FOR PLANT LOVERS

AUSTRALIA

Ivy Muse
1250 High Street, Armadale, Victoria,
Australia 3143
ivymuse.com.au

Little Leaf Co
4 / 496 Marmion Street,
Myaree, Western Australia 6154
littleleafco.com.au

Loose Leaf
31 Sackville St / Collingwood VIC 3066
looseleafstore.com.au

~

BRASIL

Jardin Plantas e Flores
Rua General Jardim
490 Centro - São Paulo
jardin.eco.br

~

DENMARK

Kaktus København
Jægersborggade 35 / 2200 København
kaktuskbh.dk

Planteplaneter
Shop Nørrebro:
Stefansgade 12 / 2200 København
planteplaneter.dk

FRANCE

Girls & Roses
32 Rue Montorgueil / 75001 Paris
girlsandroses.com

The Green Factory
17 Rue Lucien Sampaix / 75010 Paris
greenfactory.fr

Ikebanart
49 Rue Lucien Sampaix / 75010 Paris
ikebanart.com

Mama Petula
82 Avenue Denfert-Rochereau
75014 Paris
mamapetula.com

Les Mauvaises Graines
Corner BHV MARAIS
52 Rue de Rivoli7 / 75004 Paris
lesmauvaisesgraines.paris

Les Succulents Cactus
111 Rue de Turenne / 75003 Paris
lescactus.com

~

GERMANY

Blumencafé
Schönhauser Allee 127a
10437 Berlin
blumencafe-berlin.de

Goldregen Floraldesign
Lütticher Straße 49
50674 Cologne
goldregen-floraldesign.de

Hallesches Haus
Tempelhofer Ufer 1
10961 Berlin
hallescheshaus.com

Marly Lennox
The Store x Soho House Berlin
Torstrasse 1
10119 Berlin
marylennox.de

~

GREAT BRITAIN

Botany
5 Chatsworth Road
London E5 0LH
botanyshop.co.uk

Conservatory Archives
493-495 Hackney Road
London E2 9ED / United Kingdom
conservatoryarchives.co.uk

~

NEW ZEALAND

Bio Attic
62 Ponsonby Road, Grey lynn
1011 Auckland
bioattic.co.nz

Mama Petula / Paris

Wildernis / Amsterdam

THE NETHERLANDS

De Balkonie
Jan Evertsenstraat 90H
1056 EG Amsterdam
debalkonie.nl

Plantaardig
Zusterstraat 10
4331 KJ Middelburg
plantaardigmiddelburg.nl

Stek de Stadstuinwinkel
Nieuwe Binnenweg 195b
3021 GA Rotterdam
stekrotterdam.nl

Wildernis
Bilderdijkstraat 165F
1053 KP Amsterdam
wildernisamsterdam.nl

SOUTH AFRICA

Opus
The Woodstock Foundry
170 Albert Rd, Woodstock
Cape Town, 8001
opusstudio.co.za

SPAIN

Cacto Cacto
Calle Fernando VI, 7
28004 Madrid
cacto-cacto.com

Espai Joliu
Carrer Badajoz 95
08005 Barcelona
espaijoliu.tumblr.com

TURKEY

Labofem
Akat mah. / Meydan Cad 4/1
34335 Etiler/Istanbul
labofem.com

USA

Fern Shop Cincinnati
6040 Hamilton Ave
Cincinnati / OH 45224
fern-shop.com

Hot Cactus
1505.5 Echo Park Ave
Los Angeles / CA 90026
hotcactus.la

Pistils Nursery
3811 North Mississippi
Avenue Suite 1
Portland / OR 97227
pistilsnursery.com

The Sill
84 Hester Street (Chinatown)
New York / NY 10002
thesill.com

Solabee Flowers & Botanicals
801 N Killingsworth St.
Portland / OR 97217
solabeeflowers.com

ONLINESHOPS

Online airplant shop Europe + US
etairnity-airplants.com

Online plant shop Denmark
greenify.dk

Online plant shop Europe
planteplaneter.tictail.com

Online plant shop Germany
evrgreen.de

Online Terrarium & Airplants Australia
plantbypackwood.com

ACKNOWLEDGMENTS

Merci to Philippe for his ongoing support, patience and understanding,
to Judith for her design-savvy eye and creativity, to Robert for his support and good cooking,
and to all the other people who love me, support me and believe in me –
this book was possible because of you!

IGOR

A huge MERCI to Robert for his unconditional love, patience and support,
to my dear family for their enthusiasm and confidence in me, to Simone for his precious advice
and humour, to my Mastermind buddies (Anne, Catherine, Clotilde, Jane, Cécile) for their guidance,
to Philippe for his kindness and patience, and to Igor for his good vibes and all the fun
we had while creating this book.

JUDITH

And a big thank you to Lina for her amazing photography,
to Saar for the beautiful illustrations, to all the contributing bloggers for their green ideas,
and to all the homeowners who invited us into their green homes.
Last but not least, many thanks to all the Urban Jungle Bloggers
for their ongoing green creativity.

© 2021 Callwey GmbH
Klenzestraße 36, 80469 Munich
www.callwey.de
E-Mail: buch@callwey.de

13th edition 2021

The German National Library lists this publication in the German National Bibliography;
detailed bibliographic data are available in the internet at http://dnb.d-nb.de.

ISBN: 978-3-7667-2244-7

Project manager: Simone Ehmann
Copy editor, German: Bookwise, Corinna Nikolaus, Munich
Copy editor, English: Rita Forbes, Munich
Design and layout: Anna Schlecker
Illustrations: Saar Manche
Print and binding: Firmengruppe APPL, aprinta druck, Wemding

Printed in Germany

~~~~~

THE AUTHORS

Igor Josifovic is a blogger, social media expert and plant lover living between Munich and
Paris. He shares his love for interior design, travel and living with plants on his Happy Interior
Blog and with the international plant community Urban Jungle Bloggers, which he founded
together with Judith de Graaff.

Judith de Graaff is a blogger, graphic designer and plant lover, and lives with her husband and
three cats in a former factory just outside Paris. She shares her love for colour, design, travel
and living with plants on her blog JOELIX.com and with the international plant community
Urban Jungle Bloggers, which she founded together with Igor Josifovic.

~~~~~

THE PHOTOGRAPHER

Lina Skukauskė is a Lithuanian photographer focusing on hospitality and lifestyle photography subjects such as interiors, food, travel and people. She loves telling visual stories that
inspire people and capture life in a beautiful and appealing way. You can find out more about
her at www.linaskukauske.com.